THE
MESSAGE

BY TA-NEHISI COATES

The Beautiful Struggle

Between the World and Me

We Were Eight Years in Power

The Water Dancer

The Message

THE
MESSAGE

Ta-Nehisi Coates

HAMISH HAMILTON
an imprint of
PENGUIN BOOKS

HAMISH HAMILTON

UK | USA | Canada | Ireland | Australia
India | New Zealand | South Africa

Hamish Hamilton is part of the Penguin Random House group of companies
whose addresses can be found at global.penguinrandomhouse.com.

Penguin Random House UK,
One Embassy Gardens, 8 Viaduct Gardens, London SW11 7BW

penguin.co.uk
global.penguinrandomhouse.com

First published in the United States of America by One World, an imprint of Random House,
a division of Penguin Random House LLC 2024
First published in Great Britain by Hamish Hamilton 2024
001

Copyright © BCP Literary, Inc, 2024

Grateful acknowledgement is made to Beacon Press for permission to reprint three stanzas
from 'Rebirth' from *Collected Poems* by Sonia Sanchez, copyright © 2022 by Sonia Sanchez.
Reprinted with permission from Beacon Press, Boston, Massachusetts

The moral right of the author has been asserted

Printed and bound in Great Britain by Clays Ltd, Elcograf S.p.A.

The authorized representative in the EEA is Penguin Random House Ireland,
Morrison Chambers, 32 Nassau Street, Dublin D02 YH68

A CIP catalogue record for this book is available from the British Library

ISBN: 978–0–241–72418–7

Penguin Random House is committed to a sustainable future
for our business, our readers and our planet. This book is made from
Forest Stewardship Council® certified paper.

For my sons, Samori and Chris

In a peaceful age I might have written ornate

or merely descriptive books, and might have

remained almost unaware of my political loyalties.

As it is I have been forced into becoming a sort

of pamphleteer.

GEORGE ORWELL, "WHY I WRITE"

NOTES ON SOURCES

———◆ ◆———

For Notes on Sources, please visit:
ta-nehisicoates.com/the-message/notes

I.

Journalism Is Not a Luxury

Though we do not wholly believe it yet, the interior life is a real life, and the intangible dreams of people have a tangible effect on the world.

—JAMES BALDWIN

Comrades,

In the summer of 2022, I returned to Howard University to teach writing. Given my rather middling career as a university student, I couldn't help but feel somewhat sheepish about the honor. But it was an honor, because it was there that I met you. Our first class was in the woods—out in rural Virginia, where, with my friend the poet Eve Ewing, we spent two weeks reading, writing, and workshopping. I've been teaching writing in some form or capacity for almost as long as I've been a writer, and the only work I love more is writing itself. But with you I found the former rivaling the latter. I don't mean to slight any other cohort of students I've taught in other times and places—all were talented and hardworking. But the fact is, we were drawn together by something more profound.

I guess it begins with our institution, and the fact that it was founded to combat the long shadow of slavery—a shadow that we understood had not yet retreated. This meant that we could never practice writing solely for the craft itself, but must necessarily believe our practice to be in service of that larger emancipatory mandate. This was often alluded to, if not directly stated. All of our work dealt with the kind of small particulars of being human that literature generally deals with. But when you live as we have, among a people whose humanity is ever in doubt, even the small and particular—especially the small and particular—becomes political. For you there can be no real distance between writing and politics. And when I saw that in you, I saw myself.

A love of language, of course, is the root of this self. When I was barely six months old, I would crawl over to my father's speakers when he played the Last Poets. And when the record ended, I would cry until he played it again. At five I would lie on my bed, with the *Poems and Rhymes* volume of the Childcraft series splayed open to "The Duel," and all day I could not help but to murmur to myself, "The gingham dog and the calico cat / Side by side on the table sat." I did this for no other reason than the way the words felt in my mouth and fell on my ears. Later I discovered that there were MCs—human beings seemingly born and reared for the sole purpose of matching the music of language to an MPC snare or 808 kick—and the ensuing alchemy felt as natural to me as a heartbeat:

I haunt if you want, the style I possess
I bless the child, the earth, the gods and bomb the rest

Haunt. You've heard me say this word a lot. It is never enough for the reader of your words to be convinced. The goal is to *haunt*—to have them think about your words before bed, see them manifest in their dreams, tell their partner about them the next morning, to have them grab random people on the street, shake them and say, "Have you read this yet?" That was what I felt whenever I heard Rakim spit, or for that matter the Last Poets. That was the thing that had me murmuring lines from Childcraft. This affliction was enchantment and desire. It was pleasure but also a deep need to understand the mechanics of that pleasure, the math and color behind words, and all the emotions they evoked. I imagine there are children who see a painting and cannot get the image out of their minds. I imagine they turn it over alone at night in the dark, haunted, considering and reconsidering, and a small secret ecstasy grows in them each time they do this, and, just behind this, a need to convey an ecstasy all their own. I was like that from the moment I could inscribe words into memory. And this instinct naturally linked to the world around me, because I lived in a house overflowing with language organized into books, most of them concerned with "the community," as my mother would put it. And so it was made clear to me that words could haunt not only in form, not only in their rhythm and roundness, but in their content.

When I was seven years old, my mother purchased a copy of *Sports Illustrated* for me. She taught me to read before I entered school, and encouraged the practice however she could. And what more encouragement could there be than this issue of *Sports Illustrated,* which featured my hero, Tony Dorsett, running back for the Dallas Cowboys. This was 1983, an era of American football when running backs seemed as large as champions pulled out of Greek myth. How could a man of Earl Campbell's might move so fast, racing past one defender and then staving in the chest of another? How could Eric Dickerson run so high, against all convention, bounding through holes in the defense, an obvious target that was never caught? These days I will occasionally watch an old clip of Roger Craig, through will alone, breaking off a forty-six-yard run against the Rams, or Marcus Allen reversing field in the Super Bowl. But back then, in an unwired world, stories, words, histories—none of it could be gotten on demand. If you bore witness to such a feat—as I did with Allen—it lived in memory until the broadcast gods decided you could see it again. And so a magazine featuring the exploits of one of these heroes was not just, to me, an assembly of words and stories. It was a treasure.

Because I really did believe that Tony Dorsett was magic. He was five foot eight, built ordinary as one of my uncles. But when he slid the lone-starred helmet over his head, he transformed into something untouchable. I remember him darting through the defense, shifting direction at full speed, dancing, sprinting the length of the field, and outrunning an entire team. But whatever my affinity for Dorsett, this is not what I remember about that issue. In fact, until a few months ago, I'd forgotten that Dorsett was even on the cover at all, because deeper in the magazine, I found a story so unsettling, so horrific even, that it blotted out every adjacent detail.

The story was titled "Where Am I? It Has to Be a Bad Dream." Its subject was Darryl Stingley, who'd once been a wide receiver. I thought of wide receivers as mythical too—contortionists like Wes Chandler, extending back to snag a ball bouncing off into the ether, or acrobats like Lynn Swann, dancing in the air. I absorbed these exploits on Sunday mornings through highlights curated by the NFL itself. But a magazine like *Sports Illustrated* existed beyond the garden, out in the street where journalism and literature collided. And out there was neither magic nor myth—only the realest of monsters.

And so I read the true story of Stingley, who back in 1978 took a hit on a slant route and woke up in a hospital. The story began there, in the hospital—with Stingley unable to move a single limb, unable to call to his mother or wipe the tears running down his face. In an instant, the contortionist had been rendered quadriplegic. Only a few paragraphs in, I wanted to put the magazine down forever, to escape the story, but I was held fast by forces I could not then understand. I knew that there was something different in the storytelling, something in its style, that pulled me toward it with the gravity of a star, until I was there, I was on the field, yelling, pleading with Stingley to watch out for the incoming hit, and then in the hospital, right next to him, helpless to relieve the horror blooming in his eyes as he realized his fate. And then the star became a black hole, and I crossed an event horizon where I was no longer imagining myself there with Stingley, but was Stingley himself, and it was my body pinned to the bed, and the spokes were drilled into my skull, and it was I crying out to a heedless god.

I haunt if you want, the style I possess. And I was haunted—by a style, by language. And, dimly, instinctually, I understood that the only exorcism lay in more words. I went to my father and bombarded him with questions, because that was the kind of child I was, always (to the annoyance of my siblings) asking *why*. My father's way of dealing with this was patented and that day he executed the maneuver to perfection. He led me to the back room, where he kept a large collection of books, and pulled one down from the shelf. The book was *They Call Me Assassin*. It was the memoir of Jack Tatum—the defensive back who'd laid the crushing hit on Stingley.

And so I delved deeper—hoping for some insight into the mindset of a man who had permanently crippled another. I'd like to tell you I found some great revelation here, but the book was mostly filled with stories of Tatum's only vaguely interesting football career. I recall Tatum writing that the hit on Stingley was unremarkable in its violence. If a reader came, as I did, looking for some profound meditation on a catastrophe, it was not to be found. And so I was left again to grapple on my own—no Google, no Wikipedia, no social network through which to commiserate with others. Just me and this terrible story of an acrobat entombed in his own body playing over and over in the back of my mind.

But something had happened to me in this process. As a reader, I changed. I was no longer merely turning words over in my head or on my tongue—I was now turning over entire stories. Even Tatum's story spoke volumes by not speaking much at all, for it nodded to the shame one might feel or the paradox of a game that valorizes violence and then is horrified by its consequences. I did not yet see all of that. But for years after, as I turned the stories over in my mind, I could feel the revelations spinning out of them. What I felt then was that the story of Darryl Stingley broke some profound invisible law of justice, one that reigned in all my cartoons. I knew football was violent—it was the violence that backlit Tony Dorsett's escape act. But violence was the antagonist in a story with a happy ending. It could never win, could it?

But all around me violence actually was winning. That was the year when I first remember a child being shot over a trendy article of clothing; stories like that would soon become the background of my adolescence. And now danger swirled all around me—tales of razors slipped into candy apples, four-year-olds impaled with lawn darts. Stingley's story pulled all this together and illuminated a new idea: Evil did win, sometimes— maybe most times. Bad things did happen, if only for the simple reason that they could. Disturbing as this knowledge was, it made me stronger because it made me wiser. And the weight of this wisdom was intimately associated with the method of its delivery. Journalism. Personal narrative. Testimony. Stories.

I grew older. Bad things began to happen to me and the people around me: beatdowns, bankings, tool pop- pings, jewel runnings. I think the only way I ultimately survived was through stories. Because as much as stories could explain my world, they could also allow me to escape into others. And so whatever was outside, I could come back home to the *World Book Encyclopedia* and let words transport me to forests and jungles, taiga and tun- dra. Or I could pick up a copy of *Deadly Bugs and Killer Insects* and, through words, take pleasure in the lethal biology of black widows and fire ants. Or I could open up *African Glory* and cross the Sahara with Mansa Musa or see the realm of Songhai through Askia the Great. Or I could come back to my world, through LP or tape, through "Louder Than a Bomb," "The Symphony," or "My Philosophy." None of these worlds were separate in my mind. I did not have then, and do not have now, a real sense of "high" or "low" art. All I cared about was what haunted me and why—and slowly I began to see the thread running through each of them. In high school, I read *Macbeth* and found myself as far beyond the classroom as any Kool G Rap verse could take me:

SECOND MURDERER
I am one, my liege,
Whom the vile blows and buffets of the world
Hath so incens'd, that I am reckless what I do
To spite the world.

FIRST MURDERER
                    And I another,
So weary with disasters, tugg'd with fortune,
That I would set my life on any chance,
To mend it, or be rid on 't.

What I saw here was my city, which was connected to other cities whose mores and codes were then being rhapsodized in mixtapes and music videos—Gods and Earths, Gangstas and Queens. But here was another dead star, with another gravity, pulling me across centuries, until I saw that even there the rules and mores, which I had taken to be ours alone, still held. And through words I understood that my Baltimore was not damned, that what I saw in the eyes of the boys there, what I heard in the music, was in fact something old, something ineffable, which marked all of humanity, stretching from Stratford upon Avon to the Streets.

And always at these moments I was taken back to the obsessions of my childhood: the organization of words, silences, and sound into stories. And to that I added the employment of particular verbs, the playful placement of punctuation, and the private ecstasy it all brought to me. And I saw, considering the phrase "I am one, my liege, / Whom the vile blows and buffets of the world," that there was magic in Shakespeare's repetition of a sound represented in the *b,* and that this was the same magic used by Rakim, only this time with the sound represented by the *r:*

I'm the arsenal, I got artillery, lyrics are ammo
Rounds of rhythm, then I'ma give 'em piano

I was about your age when I began to understand what I had first glimpsed in that copy of *Sports*

Illustrated—that sound and rhythm are even more powerful when organized into narrative. That is to say, words are powerful, but more so when organized to tell stories. And stories, because of their power, demanded rigorous reading, interpretation, and investigation. There I was, the *Sports Illustrated* spread in my lap, feeling launched on a voyage of discovery. I finished the article but needed to know more. So I sought to report, and thus turned my own father into my first source. That source then sent me to the library to research. And there, frustratingly, the journey ended. Books could take me only so far. If only I could have talked to Tatum or Stingley myself. If only I could be the one crafting the questions and organizing and interpreting the answers and then, with words, expressing the meaning I extracted from the quest.

As it happened, I could. At Howard, I found a sprawling library beyond the single room of my father. There were databases filled with articles from magazines and newspapers. And I was an adult now, and I could, as it turned out, call people and question them myself, so that the ranks of potential sources now increased. Armed with those raw sources and my own sense of how words might be organized—*a style I possessed*—maybe I could go from the haunted to the ghost, from reader to writer, and I too could have the stars, and their undeniable gravity, at my disposal.

It was clear that such power must serve something beyond my amusement—that it should do the work of illuminating, of confronting and undoing, the violence I saw around me, that beauty must be joined to politics, that style possessed must meet struggle demanded:

> The good to be sought and the evil to be shunned were flung in the balance and weighed against each other. On the one hand there stood slavery, a stern reality glaring frightfully upon us, with the blood of millions in its polluted skirts, terrible to behold, greedily devouring our hard earnings and feeding himself upon our flesh. Here was the evil from which to escape.
>
> On the other hand, far away, back in the hazy distance where all forms seemed but shadows under the flickering light of the north star, behind some craggy hill or snow-capped mountain, stood a doubtful freedom, half frozen, and beckoning us to her icy domain.

This is Frederick Douglass breathing life into the abstract dyad of slavery and freedom—particularly the latter. Slavery is obviously evil. But to pursue the "good," the enslaved must forsake the very real land of their birth for a dream and maybe a nightmare—an "icy domain" that looms "in the hazy distance" under "flickering light . . . half frozen." Douglass's freedom is not banners or anthems, but terror that he nonetheless embraced. The contrast—the bright good of freedom in principle, set against the dark unknown reality—evokes the cliché "the devil you know." But Douglass's chiaroscuro of language illuminates the truth buried in the cliché so that we are drawn closer to a distant experience, and Douglass is thus not a stock character called "slave," but a human like us. To write like this, to imagine the enslaved, the colonized, the conquered as human beings has always been a political act. For Black writers it has been so often employed that it amounts to a tradition—one that I returned to that summer in Virginia with you.

I think this tradition of writing, of drawing out a common humanity, is indispensable to our future, if only because what must be cultivated and cared for must first be seen. And what I see is this: a figure standing at the edge of a sprawling forest tasked with mapping that forest with such precision that anyone who sees the map will feel themselves transported into the territory. The figure can see the snowy peaks in the distance and might conjure some theories as to what lies between them and those peaks—pine trees, foothills, a ravine with a stream running through it. The figure is you, the writer, an idea in hand, notes scribbled on loose-leaf, maybe an early draft of an outline. But to write, to draw that map, to pull us into the wilderness, you cannot merely stand at the edge. You have to walk the land. You have to see the elevation for yourself, the color of the soil. You have to discover that the ravine is really a valley and that the stream is in fact a river winding south from a glacier in the mountains. You can't know any of this beforehand. You can't "logic" your way through it or retreat to your innate genius. A belief in genius is a large part of what plagues us, and I have found that people widely praised for the power of their intellect are as likely to illuminate as they are to confound. "Genius" may or may not help a writer whose job is, above all else, to clarify.

A world made clear—that is what I felt at seven years old when the true face of football clarified before me. Freed from the biased curation of powerful parties, I now directly saw the sport's terrible price. I am writing in the wake of #MeToo, which was, among everything else, a movement birthed by words. For it is one thing to sketch a world where "sexual assault is a problem in the

TA-NEHISI COATES

workplace" and quite another to detail Manhattan offices with rape doors, or star anchors ambushing assistants on vacation, or actors who claim to be "male feminists" but leave a trail of abuse behind them. What I remember in reading the investigative pieces on these cases is how all the activist and academic jargon—all the talk of "patriarchy" and "rape culture" and "male privilege"—became solid and embodied in a way that did not just leave me convinced but implicated me. It was not news to me that I was privileged, as a man, but I now felt that privilege with new horror. I thought about my own career and understood that whatever its challenges, a rape button did not rank among them. And that is the world made clear:

> The quality of light by which we scrutinize our lives has direct bearing upon the product which we live, and upon the changes which we hope to bring about through those lives. It is within this light that we form those ideas by which we pursue our magic and make it realized.

Audre Lorde was writing about poetry, but I think her words apply across all arenas of writing. You cannot act upon what you cannot see. And we are plagued by dead language and dead stories that serve people whose aim is nothing short of a dead world. And it is not enough to stand against these dissemblers. There has to be something in you, something that hungers for clarity. And you will need that hunger, because if you follow that path, soon enough you will find yourself confronting not just their myths, not just their stories, but your own. This is difficult, if only because so much of our myth-making was done in service of liberation, in doing whatever we could to dig our way out of the pit into which we were cast. And above us stand the very people who did the casting, jeering, tossing soil into our eyes and yelling down at us, "You're doing it wrong." But we are not them, and the standards of enslavers, colonizers, and villains simply will not do. We require another standard—one that sees the sharpening of our writing as the sharpening of our quality of light. And with that light we are charged with examining the stories we have been told, and how they undergird the politics we have accepted, and then telling new stories ourselves.

The systems we oppose are systems of oppression, and thus inherently systems of cowardice. They work best in the dark, their essence tucked away and as unexamined as the great American pastime was once to me.

But then a writer told me a story and I saw something essential and terrible about the world. All our conversations of technique, of rhythm and metaphor, ultimately come down to this—to the stories we tell, to the need to haunt, which is to say to make people feel all that is now at stake.

When we last spoke it was the Fall semester, almost two years ago. During a light moment, I promised you that I would submit my own essay for the next workshop. You were giddy, in no small part, to turn my own lessons against me—to point out where I was vague, verbose, or just lazy. But when the semester ended, I had produced no essay. It seems I was still that middling student from thirty years ago. But the essay was real—so real that I have not seen you since. I've been traveling—Senegal, South Carolina, Palestine. But I'm home now, and with me I bring my belated assignment—notes on language and politics, on the forest, on writing. I've addressed these notes directly to you, though I confess that I am thinking of young writers everywhere whose task is nothing less than doing their part to save the world.

II.

—◆ ◆—

On Pharaohs

WHEN i stepped off the stage i knew i was home
had been here before had been away
roaming the cold climate of my mind where
winter and summer hold the same temperature
of need.

and I held up my hands. face. cut by the northern
winds and blood oozed forth kissed the place
of my birth and the sun and sea gather round
my offering and we were one as night is surely day
when you truly understand the need one has for the
    other.

a green smell rigid as morning
stretched like a young maiden 'cross the land
and I tasting a new geography took off my shoes
let my feet grow in the new dance of growth
and the dance was new and my thighs
burning like chords
left a trail for others to follow when
they returned home as all must surely do to make
past future tense.

SONIA SANCHEZ, "REBIRTH"

The other day, as I was packing for my trip to Dakar, my mother texted me a copy of one of her old sketches. This seemed appropriate, in that the sketch gave me a moment to reflect on why this long-deferred trip so weighed on me and how that long deferral related to some of my earliest notions of imagination and art. It's true that I grew up in a house of words—articles, books, lyrics. And it's true that writing took hold of me young and held me in its orbit, but there were many moons pulling at the tides of my mind. My father kept a modest and motley collection of revolutionary art—pencil sketches of pharaohs, afro-absurdist sculptures, Harlem Hellfighters captured in lithograph. In almost every house we ever lived in, he built a display of Wheaties boxes, potato chip packages, and bags of cookies, unopened, much as a toy collector might keep an original Barbie or a vintage G.I. Joe. These too were works of revolutionary art, because all these packages featured Black people, and none of them in the shuffling and shucking style that so plagued my parents' youth.

As for my mother, I think, in some other life she would have been an artist. She is a graceful dancer. She loves music. I see her now as she was then, in her short natural and thick glasses, pushing her silver Volkswagen Rabbit down Liberty Heights, tapping the wheel and singing to the Pointer Sisters: "Well, Romeo and Juliet / Samson and Delilah / baby you can bet . . ." I heard it all in that car or on the turntables at home—Prince, Nina Simone, Carmen McRae, the Platters, the Drifters, John Coltrane, Jerry Butler, Taj Mahal, Joan Armatrading. My mother has an innate sense for craft, too. I have warm memories of the two of us at the kitchen table with Scotch Tape, index cards, scissors, Elmer's paste, and wire hangers, all in service of science fair tri-folds, art class collages, or dioramas of history. She took up drawing for a while, and I would find her sketch pads scattered throughout the house. And now, all these years later, she'd found a forgotten one, too—and in it a portrait of my father, sitting sideways in a chair, his legs crossed, a fisherman's cap on his head and a book in his hand. At the top of the sketch there was a handwritten caption—"Daddy reads all the time"—and another at the bottom—"Daddy says he reads to learn." The captions were mine.

My father thinks he can fix the date of the sketch's creation. It is long before your time—1978. He is five years out of the Black Panther Party, and it is now clear that the revolution will not be televised, because the revolution will not be happening at all. We live in a row house up on Park Heights, which my parents rent by the week, and making that weekly rent is the hardest thing they will ever do. My father has worked all kinds of jobs—training guard dogs, handling bags at the airport, and now, down at the docks, unloading salt boats. But this day, the day of the portrait, he has been told that there has been some sort of misunderstanding with the union and he will not be paid. He comes home with the weight of it all upon him. He is thirty-two, and maybe now he can feel the dread that strikes you at that age—a realization that the years really can slip away, like all those dreams of revolution, without leaving a trace. And his response to all that weight is incredible: He picks up a book. *Daddy says he reads to learn.* But what was Daddy trying to learn?

I think if he tried to describe the forces shaping his life, my father would see his own actions first: his credits, his mistakes. But if he widened the aperture to the world around him, he would see that some people's credits earned them more, and their mistakes cost them less. And those people who took more and paid less lived in a world of iniquitous wealth, while his own people lived in a world of terrifying want. And what my father would have also seen is that he was confronted not just by the yawning chasm between wealth and want, but by the stories that sought to inscribe that chasm as natural. He would have pointed to the arsenal of histories, essays, novels, ethnographies, teleplays, treatments, and monographs, which were not white supremacy itself but its syllabus, its corpus, its canon.

The weight of my first trip to Africa—the many years it took me to actually go—is directly tied to that canon and to the work of its luminaries, men like Josiah Nott, a nineteenth-century anthropologist, epidemiologist, and student of civilization. Nott was also a slaveholder, which meant that he profited from the trade and labor of the people he enslaved and then profited again by his chosen field of study. "My Niggerology, so far from harming me at home, has made me a greater man than I ever expected to be," Nott wrote to his mentor, the anthropologist Samuel Morton, in 1847. "I am the big gun of the profession here." That profession had but one aim—assembling all the knowledge Nott could summon to prove we were inferior and thus fit for enslavement.

It may seem strange that people who have already attained a position of power through violence invest so much time in justifying their plunder with words. But even plunderers are human beings whose violent ambitions must contend with the guilt that gnaws at them when they meet the eyes of their victims. And so a story must be told, one that raises a wall between themselves and those they seek to throttle and rob.

When I was a boy, back in Baltimore, it was never enough for some kid who wanted to steal your football, your Diamondback dirt bike, or your Sixers Starter jacket to just do it. A justification was needed: "Shorty, lemme see that football," "Somebody stole my lil cousin bike just like that one," "Ay yo, that look like my Starter." Debating the expansive use of the verb "see," investigating the veracity of an alleged younger cousin, or producing a receipt misses the point. The point, even at such a young age, was the suppression of the network of neurons that houses the soft, humane parts of us.

For men like Nott, who sought not to plunder toys or kicks but whole nations, the need was manifestly greater. It was not just the conscience of the enslaver that had to be soothed but multiple consciences beyond his: the slave drivers and slave breakers, slave hunters and slave ship captains, lords and congressmen, kings and queens, priests, presidents, and everyday people with no real love for the slave but with human eyes and human ears nonetheless. For such a grand system, a grand theory had to be crafted and an array of warrants produced, all of them rooted in a simple assertion of fact: The African was barely human at all.

Josiah Nott looked out at the world and saw great land masses, and to each he assigned a race and to each race he pinned an exclusive ancestor whose descendants were fit to rule or be ruled. "The grand problem," he wrote, "is that which involves the common origin of races; for upon [it] hang[s] not only certain religious dogmas, but the more practical question of the equality and perfectibility of races."

The problem of "common origin" was the problem of "common humanity," and common humanity invalidated the warrant for African enslavement. For if we were all descended from the same parent, why, then, was one branch made solely for enslavement? This want of a specific warrant to plunder specific humans is as old as "race" itself. In fact, it is the whole reason race was invented. Africans had to either be excised from humanity or cast into the lower reaches to justify their exploitation. But evidence for this banishment has been generally wanting, while proof of the contrary is everywhere around us.

In 1799, the French invaded Egypt and beheld the splendor of a civilization older than Greece or Rome. Egyptology was born, and became a sensation, rolling across Europe like a wave, crashing into America in the antebellum years, just as slavery was reaching its apex. Nott was enthralled with Ancient Egypt. His collaborator, George Gliddon, separately referred to it as "the origin of every art and science known in antiquity." But Egypt was in Africa—that continent Niggerologists deemed a font of slaves—and this immediately raised uncomfortable questions. "It has been the fashion to quote the Sphinx, as an evidence of the Negro tendencies of ancient Egyptians," Morton wrote to his protégé Nott. "They take his wig for woolly hair—and as the nose is off, of course it is *flat*. But even if the face (which I fully admit) has a strong African cast, it is an almost solitary example, against 10,000 that *are not African*."

Nott and Gliddon dedicated their lives to clearing up any confusion about the racial composition of Egyptians. They authored the treatise *Types of Mankind,* which sought, among other things, to cleanse Ancient Egypt of any taint of Blackness. "For many centuries prior to the present," the two wrote incredulously, "the Egyptians were reputed to be Negroes, and Egyptian civilization was believed to have descended the Nile from Ethiopia!" When the record failed to support a total absence of "Negroes" from Egypt, Nott and Gliddon put them where they needed them. "It must be conceded that Negroes, at no time within the reach even of monumental history, have inhabited any part of Egypt," they wrote, "save as captives." This was, quite literally, an incredible coincidence—a society some thousands of years gone, organized exactly in the same manner as Nott's plantations. But for Nott, Black enslavement in Ancient Egypt was not just a coincidence, it was a warrant:

> The monuments of Egypt prove, that Negro races have not, during 4000 years at least, been able to make one solitary step, in Negro-Land, from their savage state; the modern experience of the United States and the West Indies confirms the teachings of monuments and of history; and our remarks . . . hereinafter, seem to render fugacious all proba-

bility of a brighter future for these organically-inferior types.

Long after Nott and Gliddon were gone, the idea of a Black Egypt—which by their lights meant any Egypt with a meaningful unenslaved population that resembled the enslaved population of America—haunted their progeny. In 1896, the famed educator Samuel Train Dutton insisted that Indigenous Americans and Blacks were fit only for an education worthy of the "heathen and the savage" so that they could be prepared for a life of manual labor. Key to Dutton's project was ensuring that schools teach "how the ancient Egyptians differed from the Negro, and why." In 1928, Egyptologist Arthur Weigall devoted a chapter of his *Personalities of Antiquity* to the Pharaoh Piankhi, which he entitled "The Exploits of a Nigger King."

In all this contortion and comedy, we, watching from the margins, saw a weapon. "We need not resort to any long-drawn arguments to defend negro-Ethnography against the Notts and Gliddons of our day," wrote Black nationalist James Theodore Holly in 1859. "Let them prove, if they can, to the full satisfaction of their narrow souls and gangrened hearts, that the Black faced, woolly haired, thick lipped and flat nosed Egyptians of ancient times did not belong to the same branch of the human family that those negroes do who have been the victims of the African Slave-trade for the past four centuries."

That was how I got my African name—"Ta-Nehisi," a designation in Ancient Egyptian for the kingdom of Nubia, sometimes translated as "Land of the Blacks." I was born into what the historian St. Clair Drake calls the "vindicationist tradition," that is, to Black people who sought to reclaim the very history weaponized against them and turn it back against their tormentors. If a "Black Egypt" was what the Niggerologists feared, then we would insist on its truth and take it to its logical conclusion: We were born not to be slaves but to be royalty. That explains our veneration of Black pharaohs and African kingdoms. The point was to tell a different story than the one imposed on us—an understandable response, but one that I've never made peace with.

The truth is, I never felt fitted to my name. Its length and complexity draw attention and counter my desire to live quietly in the cut. It isn't pronounced as it's written, thus forcing me into a constant dance, where I first correct people and then assure them that it's not their fault. The awkwardness was part of the point: My parents meant to mark me as a citizen of a country far different from the one in which I lived; my name was an artifact of a forgotten world and an aspiration for one yet to come. But what exactly are those worlds? My name is not meant simply to evoke a historical entity but to conjure the idea of a Black civilization—which is to say human beings filed away in a hierarchy of nobles, seers, commoners, and slaves who through their construction of monuments, recording of literature, and waging of war can rightfully be considered full human beings. But I think human dignity is in the mind and body and not in stone. And I think the moment we root our worth in castes and kingdoms, in "civilization," we have accepted the precepts of those whose whole entire legacy is the burning and flooding of a planet. And then we have already lost.

I am trying to urge you toward something new— not simply against their myths of conquest, but against the urge to craft your own. But this is a negative proposition—a description of what should not be, but not what should be—and it creates an absence in the place of a myth. How do we fill the void? For even as I left the myth of utopic African origin, I still felt something—a sense that I could not die without going home. And I felt this even knowing that that appellation— "home"—was not a fact but a need, a wish, a dream.

———◆ ◆———

Before I left for Dakar, I saved the sketch of my father on my phone. I found myself studying it in the days before my trip and even on the flight. *What was Daddy trying to learn?* My answer to that question is embarrassing. But it began forming in my mind at roughly the same moment my flight descended out of the clouds and I got my first look at the rooftops rising up from Dakar and the water rippling white against the beach. I had traveled enough in my life to be familiar with the amazement that comes upon you when the country becomes real. You look down and are shocked to see the mountains near the city rising to meet you or the ocean around the island turning green. But not once, in all my time, have I ever felt the mix of joy, dread, and hope that I felt as that flight descended. Maybe you've already done this yourself and felt this same weight. I know that some of you were born on the Continent, and thus these words will hit different. All I can say is that when I saw the city below, all I could do was mutter to myself the only words that could approach the feeling coursing through me, and the words were:

"Oh, shit."

The flight landed, and after the rituals of deboarding and customs I found myself in the back of a car being driven into the city. What I remember with the most clarity from that first drive is a dim fear that became more legible as the highway opened into *la Corniche,* the long beach along the Atlantic. All along that beach I saw what looked like the abandoned remnants of an outdoor training gym—bench presses, a manual elliptical, pull-up bars. Time and the elements seemed to have gotten the best of the equipment, and in the blur of our passing I saw yellow paint peeling from the machines to reveal the rusting metal beneath. I assumed that these pieces were the remains of some public works project gone wrong, and the sight of this ostensible failure immediately became a sign of our collective dysfunction, of the "Negro race's" irredeemably savage state. And hearing that voice in my mind, I came to a terrible realization: After all the work of my parents, all the *Ashanti to Zulu* and *Bringing the Rain to Kapiti Plain,* after all the drums and dance classes, after all the African names, after the entire arsenal of vindication, I was still afraid that the Niggerologists were right about us.

At the hotel I took a long nap, and when I finally left my room that evening and walked onto the beach just outside, I felt out of sorts. I saw parents sprawled in beach chairs and kids happily splashing in the water. Between my room and the hotel restaurant, there was a pool whose coping was flush with the water's surface so that when swimmers emerged, it appeared as if they had emerged from the ground itself. Not far from the pool, a DJ was setting up his rig while a bartender mixed drinks. At the sight of this bartender, I felt a pinhole of sadness open in me. Inside the restaurant the vibe was cosmopolitan—men in long flowing boubous, women in head wraps, and others with sunglasses pulled up like headbands. Wine and champagne flowed. Now the pinhole widened, and I wondered if this was just the loneliness of being so far from loved ones and home. But I hadn't been gone a full day.

I ordered dinner, and for the first of many times in my trip, I looked out on the Atlantic Ocean, now mere feet away. From my table, I could see the waves breaking gently against the beach. A memory from the other side now washed over me: I am ten and with my mother in Berlin, Maryland—at the far end of the state's eastern shore. On this trip we are staying with my Aunt Toppy and my Uncle Melvin. We visit cousins and other aunts and uncles, all of whom seem to live along the same small country road. Then we drive to the ocean, and I take a blue-and-yellow inflatable raft and wade out into the breakers, away from America. And now, decades later, here I am staring back from the other side.

I felt the sadness now increase, expanding from a pinhole until it was wide as the sea itself, rippling with each wave that crested and fell on this African shore. I had traveled back to a kind of Big Bang. A universe would be born on the other side of the water, but first countless worlds would have to die. And I realized I was sad, not because I was alone but because I was not. I had indeed come home, and ghosts had come back with me.

When I woke up the next morning, the weight of it all, the sadness, the fear, it was all still there. A sliver of light peeked through the shades. I did not want to move. But I know how sadness can exert its own gravity, growing more powerful the longer it holds you. So I got up and got dressed and paid a driver to take me into town, resolved to see the reality of this home that I did not know.

Dakar moved slow around me, like the people and the great heat that fell over this city had reached an understanding. I perceived this slowness of movement even as I felt my mind trying to catch up. The most banal details opened into a world of questions. A truck would speed by with men hanging off the side, and I would find myself wondering if anyone ever fell and if that would cause the men to rethink the practice. I would watch as old ladies crammed into public buses with dented fenders, and I would wonder where the line ended. And there was so much commerce—stands and stands of men selling T-shirts or a kind of fried bread or other foods and objects. There was something steam-punk about it all—a fusion of the traditions of the old and the machinery of the new. Men sat on old stoops with huge construction projects looming in the distance. Scenes of breakdown and grace interwove. Women sold slices of watermelon across from collapsed buildings on roads littered with rusted cans. I stood on a street with potholes filled with water, trying to guess at the depths, until my eyes were drawn to a man wearing the most beautiful tailored suit I'd ever seen.

I hadn't noticed it yet, but the ghosts were no longer talking. The sea of sadness closed in on itself, and now I felt like a child again, filled with questions about the smallest details of the world around me. I was trying very hard to hide the wonder behind my eyes, because I knew that would mark me as a tourist, and tourists were targets. I failed. A man yelled to me: "Hey! Hey!" And when I turned, I saw him smiling through missing teeth. He said, "I love Chicago!" I smiled back. He walked over and shook my hand. "Hey," he said, our hands still clasped. "I lived in Chicago! I love America!" The old street sense came over me, and I felt a hustle in the offing—and then surprised myself by walking right into it.

"Why are you in Dakar?"

"I wanted to see Africa."

"This is your first time?" I smiled and said yes. He waved his hands excitedly. He had a live one and he knew it, and honestly, so did I. And off we walked through the streets, until we reached a three-story building. I followed the man inside and found myself in a sea of the most beautiful fabric I'd ever seen. Gorgeous bolts of printed cloth, and shirts and dresses made from the fabric, hung from the walls of the building's tight hallways and were stacked in piles in every room we passed through. I selected a few garments and wraps. I asked how much. A man in charge looked at me and said, "This is Africa." Then he pulled out his calculator and handed it to me. He had me put in the amount I wanted to pay, and then he took the calculator back from me and typed in a counter. We went back and forth a few times until we reached an agreement. I did the rough conversion of CFA, the Senegalese currency, to dollars in my head, but I still could not tell whether I was being charged a fair price. It seemed beside the point. I walked outside, feeling rich. I tipped my guide and then went on my way.

It was time for lunch. Now alone, I found a restaurant comprised of two roughly appointed rooms. There was no real roof, save a kind of tarp pulled over the walls of the rooms for shade. I entered and stood apprehensively at the front of the first room. All the tables were occupied. I felt a jolt of electricity run through me. I have always thought of myself as an anti-thrill-seeker. I am afraid of heights. I hate roller coasters. Gambling is lost on me, as are horror movies with their jump scares. But when I'm traveling, I live for these awkward moments, when I need something, in this case to eat, but am not quite sure how to get it. There is usually an easy way out. I felt the desire to retreat to something more familiar, something designed for the tourist, maybe back at the hotel, seated by that sad ocean. But I had been here before and now knew the big thrill of small victories. And so I waited until a waitress waved and pointed at a table where a man was finishing his meal. He nodded, and I sat. A few minutes later he was gone. I managed to order in French and found myself facing a heaping plate of fish and jollof rice and a glass of sorrel. I looked around at all the people chattering with companions or eagerly eating in silence and felt the reward for pushing through a moment of uncertainty. I had, in a small way, perhaps through an anteroom, arrived.

Back at the hotel, after a nap, I got dressed for dinner. A fellow writer, Hamidou Anne, was picking me up. As we drove up *la Corniche,* the sun started to set over the ocean, and the temperature started to drop. In the cooling twilight I saw packs of people running along the beach. Again we passed the area on the beach filled with exercise equipment, but here at dusk it was bustling with men and women doing crunches, chin-ups, and dips. Beyond the machines, I saw soccer fields and basketball courts, all brimming with life. There was no disrepair or abandonment—there was only me and the notions that still haunted.

We ate at a small, quiet restaurant on the coast. A line of pebbled steps led from the dining area to the ocean. Again, my mind flashed back to the other side of this dark ocean, and I saw myself with the blue-and-yellow raft, and I felt something pulling me down to the water. And so I walked down the steps until I was right at the edge of the ocean, the water lapping against the stony shore. I bent down, and when I felt the water rush between fingers, a joy came with the cold of the wave, and I heard the ghosts singing. I don't know if I've ever experienced a deeper sense of triumph in my life. I felt that I had somehow beaten history itself. I thought of all my exponential grandmothers taken from this side of the world and into the vast ocean. I thought of their frustrated dreams of getting back home. I thought of the home they tried to make on the other side, despite it all. I carried a part of all of them with me, every one of them. And I had come back. And looking out on that rocky beach, I felt the whole of the land speak to me, and it said, *What took you so long?*

What indeed.

This is about the forest again—about the limits of genius, about the need to walk the land, as opposed to intuit and hypothesize from the edge. There are dimensions in your words—rhythm, content, shape, feeling. And so too with the world outside. The accretion of imperfect, discomfiting life must be seen and felt so that the space in your mind, gray, automatic, and square, fills with angle, color, and curve—the potholes, the dented fenders, the fried bread, the walls of fabric, the heaping plate of rice and fish. But the color is not just in the physical world you observe but in the unique interaction between that world and your consciousness—in your interpretation, your subjectivity, the things you notice in yourself. My own surprise at, say, Africans jogging on the beach or a dilapidated gym revealing itself as a beautiful example of civic spirit says something important about the world I was trying to describe but also about me, my fears, and my doubts.

The next day, I was back by the sea for lunch. I was developing a ritual wherein—even when I was alone—I took a few moments of solemn meditation. The day was perfect. Hot as usual, but already the African in me was emerging—it took the form of a comprehension of the virtues of shade and of moving slow. I came out of my meditation and ordered a plate of fish yassa, rice, and plantains. Then I watched as a group of boys on longboards paddled out into the ocean, waited for a righteous wave, mounted, and surfed back in. I see them now in my mind, lanky and long, their spider arms waving in the air, their young courage heedless of the nearby rocks. Black Americans who have traveled to Senegal will often remark on the beauty of the people. They mean this physically—that the people of Senegal are some of the most striking they've ever seen. And it's true; they are beautiful. I had to work extremely hard not to stare. Even my server that day, with her dreadlocks curling around her head like a crown, was striking in all the ways we are told to think we are not. Everywhere I went in Dakar, I was amazed—too amazed, I think. The remarking on Senegalese beauty, the tone of it, betrays a deep insecurity, a shock that the deepest and blackest part of us is really beautiful.

And this too is the shade of Niggerology. For Africa is not just the geographic origin of our ordeal; it is the anchor of the idea, the warrant, that justified the ordeal. America's master race practiced, in their words, "African slavery," and when they went to war to save this institution, they went with a story on their lips and a warrant in their hand: Slavery must endure and the races must be separated to save their "wives and daughters" from "pollution and violation" on account of "the lust of half-civilized Africans." Before that war, they had already transfigured slaveholding into the work of God, which sought to save "the African, coming from a barbarous state and from a tropical climate," and transform these captives into "the happiest set of people on the face of the globe." Teddy Roosevelt, reporting on his voyage to Africa, described a continent of "ape-like savages" whose brightest lights had only "advanced to the upper stages of barbarism" and had thus developed "a very primitive kind of semi-civilization." It was not narrow prejudice that Roosevelt wielded but something broader, a story that would make his reader understand that "progress and development in this particular kind of new land depend exclusively upon the masterful leadership of the whites." And from this foundational notion of "ape-like men," "half-civilized Africans," and "tropical barbarians," the cinematic universe of Niggerology follows: the Gold Dust Twins, Korn Kinks cereal, Niggerheads, Nigger Hair tobacco, Sambo, Uncle Ben's, Aunt Jemima, and Marse Chan—icons meant to denigrate our world and elevate theirs.

I'm thinking of Toni Morrison's Pauline about to give birth to a Black girl. I am thinking of her escape into the movies, into the stories:

There in the dark her memory was refreshed, and she succumbed to her earlier dreams. Along with the idea of romantic love, she was introduced to another—physical beauty. Probably the most destructive idea in the history of human thought. Both originated in envy, thrived in insecurity, and ended in delusion. In equating physical beauty with virtue, she stripped her mind, bound it, and collected self-contempt by the heap.

I am thinking of Pauline voicing the futility in this escape:

I 'member one time I went to see Clark Gable and Jean Harlow. I fixed my hair up like I'd seen hers on a magazine. A part on the side, with one little curl on my forehead. It looked just like her. Well, almost just like. Anyway, I sat in that show with my hair done up that way and had a good time. I thought I'd see it through to the end again, and I got up to get me some candy. I was sitting back in my seat, and I taken a big bite of that candy, and it pulled a tooth right out of my mouth. I could of cried. I had good teeth, not a rotten one in my head. I don't believe I ever did get over that. There I was, five months pregnant, trying to look like Jean Harlow, and a front tooth gone. Everything went then. Look like I just didn't care no more after that. I let my hair go back, plaited it up, and settled down to just being ugly.

Morrison presents a Black woman aspiring to white beauty but not just a vague, abstract white beauty. Jean Harlow is the anchor for Morrison's claim that "physical beauty" is "probably the most destructive idea in the history of human thought." It is a grand pronounce-ment, made grander by use of contrast: the superlative (most destructive) enhanced by the chancy (probably), like sea salt over dark chocolate.

Morrison's "probably" is irony—an understatement that understates nothing. But what grounds these ideas is the specificity of how they land in the life of Pauline, the particulars of her story and language—the part and curl in her hair, the candy breaking her tooth, the preg-nancy, and the simple, devastating declaration "every-thing went then." Here is a woman whose condition is defined by a Jim Crow order, defined still further by a Jim Crow story—"A little black girl yearns for the blue eyes of a little white girl, and the horror at the heart of her yearning is exceeded only by the evil of fulfillment."

The next night I was back out with Hamidou and his wife, Khanata, at the same outdoor restaurant with the pebbled steps leading down to the water. I walked down in the darkness and went through my new meditation ritual, this time reaching down and letting the water lap into my hand. Then I walked back up and took a seat with my hosts.

49

I ordered a beer. The ocean was now only visible when the thundering waves crashed white against the rocks. My distant dream of Africa was fading as I sat there across from two Africans, two individuals who I had come to like very much as people—their ease, their humor. We were linked by related traumas of colonialism and enslavement. But even now I am wondering what was there and what I projected, and whether this feeling of having tracked down long-lost siblings was real or imagined.

On that count we settled for humor, joking about how most Africans, who have never lived under the one-drop rule, see African Americans. The lines were blurry. LeBron James was Black. Beyoncé was mixed, despite having two Black parents by the American definition. Her husband, Jay-Z, was Black because he was a "rapper" and not a "singer." Likewise, Steph Curry—two Black parents notwithstanding—would be mixed, but he played basketball, and so was Black. His wife, though—she was mixed.

And what of me. "You're mixed, Ta-Nehisi," Khanata replied, laughing. "Look, I understand what Black is in America. I get that you're Black there, but here you are mixed. That's how we see most Black Americans."

I don't know what it says about me that I just sipped my beer and laughed. Maybe it was seeing my own gospel—the social construction of race—so dispassionately preached back at me. Maybe it was thinking back to my Black American friends and all our jokes about DNA tests and who is 100 percent African (none of us) and who is not. And then the humor faded.

Khanata pointed out that in Senegal this "mixed" look is treasured. Black Americans are seen as cool, glamorous, and even beautiful *because we are mixed.* And many of the Senegalese women take steps—from straightening hair to lightening skin—to get that "Black American/mixed" look. This did surprise me. The one-drop rule had shaped us and then reached across the ocean to shape them, so that even here in Senegal, Pauline was pining for Jean Harlow. Except the Jean Harlow was us. And as I sat there with my lost siblings, listening to Khanata, it occurred to me that the "mixed" look they treasure here is itself a marker of the ordeal, an inheritance of the mass rape that shadows all those DNA jokes I make with my friends. The valuing of light skin was obviously not new to me as a Black American, but to encounter the idea here, to know that even "back home" Pauline would not be safe, was chilling. I had come back to the origin point of all of us to see my lost siblings, the ones who had evaded sale and slavery. But, of course, the warrant had gotten there first.

The next morning I got up early and headed for the 7 A.M. shuttle that would ferry me from the mainland to the island of Gorée. I was told that the early shuttle would afford me the luxury of being in the company of as few tourists as possible. The sun was not yet up. The air was cool. I almost missed the boat because I had left my phone in my room. My driver had to rush me back to the hotel and then turn around and rush off again to the harbor. I got there just in time for the men working the boat to hustle me on board. I made a few off-color jokes to myself about the last time a group of Africans had hustled my people onto a boat. I guess I should say that this sense of Dakar as any kind of origin point for Black America is itself a story, an invention. The invention is a collective one, an origin imagined and dreamed up to fill an emptiness of a people told that they come from nothing and thus have done nothing and thus are nothing. Gorée and its alleged Door of No Return fill that need—a perfectly crafted peg for the hole in our story. But by now it was well established that very few of the reported millions of enslaved people passed through that door. I knew all that. But, here again, no amount of scholarship could have stopped me from feeling what I felt at that moment as the boat pulled away from the coast of Africa, away from home.

There was nothing particularly romantic about the waters between the mainland of Senegal and the island just off its coast. I saw big ships, tankers maybe, some in apparent disrepair or abandoned. But it was a clear, beautiful morning. There were only a few other passengers aboard our ferry. I walked up to the boat's second level, where I could be alone with the sea. And then I saw it, breaking from behind the industrial ships, a bright island dotted with houses of all kinds of colors and fronted by a stony fort. Gorée.

Every year, a group of activists descends on Alabama to replay the civil rights movement's most famous set piece of martyrdom, Bloody Sunday and the march across the Edmund Pettus Bridge. I never quite saw the point of this ritual replay of trauma. But standing on the deck of that boat, approaching the island, I finally understood. It is a pilgrimage. And now, approaching Gorée, I was a pilgrim on an ancestral journey, back to the beginning of time, not just to my own birth but to the birth of the modern world.

The island was quiet, save the few residents walking along the coast. The shops near the dock were all closed.

A lone woman watched us disembark and approached to say to me, in perfect English, that she had a shop nearby, giving the impression that she fully expected to see me before I finished my trip. I laughed and walked on. Another gentleman approached and offered to show me around. I declined and was glad I did. By then I was overrun by thoughts and emotions, and I really needed to filter through them, to understand them, and I felt the standard tour guide's litany of important places could only get in the way of the feelings I was having in this moment, a moment I never thought I even needed.

I walked south down a cobblestone road, listening to the goats bleating and roosters crowing in the distance. I felt a deep calm. And then, at the end of the street, I found a hill and climbed it, and from that vantage point I looked out at the sea. I saw the waves crashing, and the familiar sadness that I'd felt that entire trip every time I looked out into the sea came over me again. In my mind, I was traveling across an epic dating back some five hundred years, when the first of us were carried off. Entire worldviews, systems of study, political movements, wars, and literature were birthed by that one act. And such deep suffering. Standing on that hill, I felt it all personally. My mind returned to Baltimore, to the sketch, to my father trying to read his way out. The moment was broken by the island's guide—I guess I was going to get a tour whether I liked it or not. I accepted this time, allowing the experience to happen to me, conceding that the experience was not just mine. I slid him some CFA when we were done and then went to visit the woman at the market to buy some wares.

On the way back from Gorée, as the shuttle broke through the waves, for the first time I was stunned to find tears welling in my eyes. I felt ridiculous. Gorée was a mythical site of departure but still it had gotten ahold of me. I know what I have said to you—against giving meaning to such conjurations, against sentiment divorced from evidence, against a world that escapes footnotes. It's actually an empiricism that dates back to my time at Howard, in Douglass Hall, where my history professors would send me to the scholarly journals and monographs in the stacks. And too in that wider community in D.C., beyond Howard, where I found that same spirit of skepticism in the irascible poets who schooled me, who loved only one thing more than writing, and that was arguing. And then I found it again in journalism, with editors who believed that whatever magic there was in our writing was generated by the streets we walked, the quotes we took down and checked and appended to real names on the record. And I got it from my father.

There were elders in my world who took to nationalism as religion, which is to say a set of answers for both their politics and their lives. But my dad could not be pinned down. He was skeptical and irreverent and, like his patron saint Malcolm X, searching, always searching. That patented move of his, the one he pulled when I was still grappling with Darryl Stingley, where he led me back into the library and let the books talk for him, reflected his deepest faith. The answer to everything was in a book, he believed, which is to say in the record. I think back to that sketch of him. A couple months later he would be in college, and a few years after that he would be working as a research librarian. He's in his seventies now, but you can still find him sitting in his chair with a book, searching. Trying to learn.

A few weeks after I got back he called me. He'd just finished a history of the rebellion of the enslaved in eighteenth-century Guyana. He loved the book but was pained by how the rebellion concluded—not just in defeat but with its leaders turning on each other and ultimately collaborating with the very people who had enslaved them. He sighed as he recounted it to me and

said, "I don't think we are going to get back to Africa."
My father did not mean this physically. He meant the
Africa of our imagination, that glorious Eden we conjured up as exiles, a place without the Mayflower, Founding Fathers, conquistadors, and the assorted corruptions
they had imposed on us. That Africa could no longer
even be supported in his imagination because the corruption was not imposed at all but was in us, was part of
the very humanity that had been denied us. That is
where his skeptical searching landed him—not on the
shores of a lost utopia but in the cold fact of human fal-
libility. And yet here I was, on this boat from Gorée, my
eyes welling up, grieving for something, in the grips of
some feeling I am still, even as I write this, struggling to
name.

Here is what I think: We have a right to our imagined traditions, to our imagined places, and those traditions and places are most powerful when we confess that
they are imagined. Gorée is the name of a place my
people have proclaimed as sacred, a symbolic representation of our last stop before the genocide and rebirth of
the Middle Passage, before, as Robert Hayden once
wrote, our "voyage through death / to life upon these
shores." We have a right to that memory, to choose the
rock of Gorée, to consecrate it, to cry before it, to

mourn its meaning. And we have a right to imagine ourselves as pharaohs, and then again the responsibility to ask if a pharaoh is even worthy of our needs, our dreams, our imagination.

I went to Senegal in silence and solitude, like a man visiting the grave of an uncertain ancestor. Besides Hamidou, Khanata, and their darling kids, I had spent my trip alone, walking and wandering, grieving and marveling, so that the Dakar I saw was not so much a city of people but, like Gorée itself, a monument to the Last Stop before we were remade. It occurs to me now that I had come to see a part of Africa but not Africans. Indeed, almost every encounter I had with actual people found me, as I was back at Gorée, seeking out the solace of my own reflection. Toward the end of my trip, the limits of this approach were becoming clear. I began to feel there was something deeply incurious in the approach of a man who insists on walking through the rooms of his childhood home to commune with ghosts, heedless of the people making their home there now. So on my last night, Hamidou and Khanata organized a group of activists and writers to come together. I admit I did not know what to expect—of myself or them. We sat in a circle drinking tea and eating *pastel*. We went around the circle introducing ourselves in French. I managed about half the meeting before my brain tired out and had to switch to English. But there was no guilting from the group. Everyone smiled. They were my kind of people—activists against the corruption of the state, writers delving into rising homophobia. But they were something more.

We are, Black people, here and there, victims of the West—a people held just outside its liberal declarations, but kept close enough to be enchanted with its promises. We know the beauty of this house—its limestone steps, its wainscoting, its marble baths. But more, we know that the house is haunted, that there is blood in the bricks and ghosts in the attic. We know that there is both tragedy and comedy in this condition. Our own lives and culture—our music, our dance, our writing— were all crafted in this absurd space beyond the walls of "civilization." This is our collective power:

> All classes of a people under social pressure are permeated with a common experience; they are emotionally welded as others cannot be. With them, even ordinary living has epic depth and lyric intensity, and this, their material handicap, is

their spiritual advantage. So, in a day when art has run to classes, cliques and coteries, and life lacks more and more a vital common background, the Negro artist, out of the depths of his group and personal experience, has to his hand almost the conditions of a classical art.

Our own Alain Locke, the great curator of the Harlem Renaissance, called this position our "spiritual advantage," but I like the phrase he uses a paragraph later—our "vast spiritual endowment from which our best developments have come and must come." I find the highest meaning in communing with those with whom the endowment is shared, with those who well comprehend the fire that sets our words alight.

That last night sitting there, I was a writer surrounded by people who too knew the fire. They did not need to have the hypocrisies, the lies, the Niggerology explained. I knew slavery and Jim Crow, and they knew conquest and colonialism. And we were joined by an inescapable act: The first word written on the warrant of plunder is *Africa*. Someday there will be more—and I guess there already is: in Afrobeats and Amapiano. And I guess there always was: in jazz and our rituals of dap. And the lines are bending in amazing ways.

I know what I said about clarity, about mapping the shape and content of words to feeling. But I confess that I have not yet found the words to capture the linkage. Halfway through our meeting, a young woman, perhaps in her twenties, joined the party. I was sitting in a circle fielding questions. She stood at the edge of the circle with a look of amazement on her face. She took a seat next to me. I answered a few more questions from the group and then she raised her hand and asked her own. She introduced herself as Bigue Ká and told me she was a grad student at Cheikh Anta Diop University working on a dissertation about my books. I'm sure she asked a question, but I don't remember it. Now the amazement was my own: There I was on the other side, among family divided from each other by centuries. I had come back. But my own writing had gotten here first.

III.

———•—•———

Bearing the
Flaming Cross

The only book learning we ever got was when we stole it. Master bought some slaves from Cincinnati, that had worked in white folks houses. They had stole a little learning and when they came to our place they passed on to us what they knew. We wasn't allowed no paper and pencil. I learned all my A.B.C.'s without it. I knows how to read and aint never been in a school room in my life. There was one woman by the name Aunt Sylvia. She was so smart she foreknowed things before they took place.

ANONYMOUS

A few years back, when I was in Baltimore for the holidays, I found myself flipping through some of my old childhood effects. It was Christmas Day. My family had just finished eating and was preparing to gather at my sister's place around the corner for drinks, laughter, stories, and general merriment. I wandered away from the party and into a back room that was once an office for my father's small publishing company and that my

65

mother now uses for storage. There were boxes stacked and a bookshelf that held random papers and a couple of ragged black-and-white composition books that I recognized as my own. I opened one of the books and found pages covered with the chicken scratches that drove all my elementary school teachers to fits—words smashing into each other, letters collapsing down the blue lines of the page. I stopped on a page with the heading "Math." There were two lines of addition and subtraction, but the numbers, instead of finding their place in the operation, seemed to be engaged in a kind of battle royale. I flipped to another page, where I had attempted to complete an ostensibly simple task: copy a series of sentences into my notebook. I might as well have been copying Sanskrit. And there at the bottom, I saw a note written in lipstick red: "Ta-Nehisi was restless today. He had problems following directions." The page was dated 2-18-82. I was six years old, and I had already begun to suspect that something was wrong with me.

It was hard to avoid this conclusion. I was, by everyone's lights, a bright enough child. I tested well. When bored, I read on my own. Where my classmates stumbled their way through the *Weekly Reader,* I glided across multisyllabic words. But when it came to fulfilling the

basics of what school required—sitting in my chair, pay-
ing attention to directions, walking in a single file, raising my hand for the lavatory pass, packing the correct
number of pencils, sharpeners, and erasers—I could not
cope. Elementary turned to middle then high school,
pencils to pens, rulers to protractors, but my perfor-
mance was frozen in time. My report cards offered testimony about a problem child who shouldn't have
been—a kid who was seemingly "smart" and yet "restless" who "wasted time," whose "conduct" needed im-
provement and who could not "follow directions."

I've always been ashamed of this sense that I did less
with more, that I had one job and could not complete
it. Looking at those composition books reminded me of
that shame, which was connected not just to my own
vague expectations but to the more concrete objectives
laid out by my struggling parents. I wanted them to be
proud of me, and even if I did not have the words for it
back then, I felt the weight of their disappointment. I
guess I should add that I've showed those notebooks to
a few friends who have told me that the ADHD screams
off the page. Those friends are all younger than me
and—like you—were born into an era of therapy, coun-
seling, and drugs. The fact that even now, at age forty-
eight, it takes all my concentration to handwrite a

sentence within the appointed lines of my reporting notebooks, that I must write in capital letters so that the words are legible to me later, lends credence to their case. Sometimes I wonder how I got out—that is, how in god's name a child who could barely write his own name in a straight line would become a writer. I guess the obvious answer is the wonder that is the word processor. But when I was young, it was not at all clear that a coming technology might save me. School was not just a place of instruction—it was a first and last chance. Black boys who failed at school did not, from what I saw, generally go on to better things. More often, they did not go on at all.

I think that what we were being taught was less a body of knowledge than a way to be in the world: orderly, organized, attentive to direction. There is nothing wrong with developing those skills—in fact, I've learned the hard way how useful they can be. What is wrong is their fetishization, the way they were allowed to outrank the actual body of knowledge held within algebra or English lit. The result was that "learning" felt like a kind of bait and switch. And this frustrated me because I truly did love to learn—it just so happened I learned best away from my desk, where ideas and concepts could be made tangible.

I loved our field trips to the Walters Art Museum, the Maryland Science Center, or the National Aquarium. I loved projects and book reports where I was free to make the knowledge my own as I best knew how. In third grade I was placed in a science class for "gifted" children. I remember one of my early assignments: Demonstrate the concept of biological "adaptation" by imagining and crafting an animal that had evolved in response to its environment. My mother—ever the artist—purchased paint, gathered up old copies of *The Baltimore Sun,* and showed me how to make papier-mâché. So armed, I produced a sharklike fish painted different shades of blue and black to show its adaptation— the ability to change colors as it made its way through the ocean. I had learned, and so indelible was the lesson that even now, whenever I read the word "adaptation" I see my imaginary shark down there in the depths.

Even now, in my studies of foreign languages, to commit a word to memory I must see it operate in multiple sentences, associate it with an image or, better yet, a story. A few years back, I had to study seventh-grade math for research and found that I could only make the information stick by pulling the numbers out of the air and matching them with the world I knew, so that the integer −236 became a business loan, keys of coke on consignment, a sharecropper trembling at the plantation store counter. What I am saying is that, like many people, I best remember a concept when I can analyze it and place it in the real world. In this, I am fortunate to have found writing, a form that must make the abstract and distant into something tangible and felt.

I don't think I'm alone in this. Do you remember Kathryn Schulz's piece "The Really Big One" from the workshop? The subject was clear and important: A tsunami was coming that would wipe the Pacific Northwest clean. But this disaster had an arrival schedule measured in centuries. How do you engage your reader with a story of a disaster that may not happen in their lifetime or the lifetimes of anyone they know?

For Schulz the first step is relegating jargon—"plate tectonics," "continental shelf," "subduction"—to the background, because jargon makes the mind go gray. Instead, Schulz clarifies the concepts behind the jargon with the phenomena of our everyday world. In her piece, earthquakes are not just measured on a Richter scale but also by the hands of a ticking watch, and they are rendered with all the violence befitting the subject. "There was a chill in the air, and snow flurries, but no snow on the ground, nor, from the feel of it, was there ground on the ground," Schulz writes. "Trees rattle, flagpoles whip, and buildings lurch back and forth a foot at a time, digging a trench in the yard."

And then Schulz sketches the future to make us feel what we might if a tsunami struck:

> If it happens at night, the ensuing catastrophe will unfold in darkness. . . . Nonchalance will shatter instantly. So will everything made of glass. . . . Refrigerators will walk out of kitchens, unplugging themselves and toppling over. . . . Unmoored on the undulating ground, the homes will begin to collapse.

The verbs are surreal, but the shock of them, the contrast, brings the inanimate to life. The switch to the future tense gives the coming disaster the kind of inevitability that her reporting, by this time, has established as true. And then there are the clever rhythmic sentences that powerfully evoke sight and sound: "the ensuing catastrophe will unfold in darkness," or "That nonchalance will shatter instantly. So will anything made of glass."

These sentences stick with me, so that just as the word "adaptation" is attached to a creature, the phrase "seismic event" conjures glass shattering, refrigerators walking, and the ground undulating (what a beautiful word). I learned something.

Which brings me back to my struggles in school. *What was I supposed to learn?* There is the obvious answer to that question—the times tables, spelling, grammar, the facts of American history—but I'm not so sure. Every year our school system turns out straight-A students who have taken the same foreign language for years and yet can barely communicate with native speakers of that language. And that is because they do not study the language to speak it. Instead, they study the portion of the language that is most amenable to flashcards and pop quizzes: conjugations, vocabulary, declensions. This amenable portion of knowledge has great value, but removed from everyday life, it's just theory. Imagine learning to swim by reading and memorizing the steps of a front crawl but never jumping into a pool.

Why do we teach our students this way? I return to the idea that seeing the world clearly allows for clearer action. I taught "The Really Big One" for its craft because it does a hard and necessary thing: It fuses beauty and politics in a way that clarifies our view and clarifies our action. Now that I can see the full scale of this disaster and the terror that will inevitably ensue, and now that I understand this as the eventual fate of a large swath of the western coast of my country, it is natural that I also now ask what our government is doing about it.

But there are people who would prefer that that question remain unasked, that the world and its affairs be reducible to flash cards and pop quizzes. Paulo Freire wrote of the "banking" system of education, in which students are treated as receptacles for information and judged on how efficiently—how "meekly"—they "receive, memorize, and repeat" that information. A teacher delivers the student information and the student succeeds by repeating it. But the medium is the message: What is being learned by students is not just the facts they memorize but the purpose of this knowledge:

> The more students work at storing the deposits entrusted to them, the less they develop the critical consciousness which would result from their intervention in the world as transformers of that world. The more completely they accept the pas-

sive role imposed on them, the more they tend simply to adapt to the world as it is and to the fragmented view of reality deposited in them.

This makes me sad in so many ways. I feel the sadness of being back there in third grade, disappointing my teachers and parents, wondering what was wrong with me. I feel the sadness of knowing my parents and teachers were doing the best they could. And then, finally, I feel the sadness of knowing that we were all enrolled in a banking system and that, even now, there are young people laboring under this system, being told that their dreams of being a writer, or an artist, or even just an educated person, hinge on their ability to sit still in a square box, when, for so many of us, it hinges on the opposite.

I never wanted to be that sort of teacher—a banker—and it was never really an option. I was just twenty years old when I led my first writing workshops, and those sessions were conducted not in school but in a prison, the very place so many of my elders feared was my fate. I wonder what they would have said, seeing me there, teaching poetry to Black men, all of whom were older than me. I was a junior teacher, which means that the course was led by two older poets—and thank god for that. Each week one of us picked a poem, gave warm-up exercises, and led the group critique. When my turn came, I was petrified. I would have led with Larry Neal—

> After Malcolm, the seasons turned stale. There was a dullness in the air for awhile. And you had gone, and there was a lingering beauty in the pain.

—because even then I was entranced with the alchemy of beauty and events, the personal and the political. But what I remember most is the exchange. These men were Black like me, but their experiences were far from my own. I offered what little I knew about writing, and through their writing they offered me the striking stuff of their lives. Twenty-five years later, I met you, and my polarities were reversed. In that prison I was with Black men old enough to be my father. With our class, it was mostly Black women young enough to be my daughters. It didn't matter. Being in a room dominated by sisters and writers who felt safe enough to share themselves, as those brothers and writers did back in that prison workshop, proved once again that the line between teacher and student is dotted.

I don't know that this mode of teaching is applicable everywhere—I don't know that we can in all subjects be comrades. But I think many of us who are teachers and professors have forgotten that the syllabus serves the student, and all around us are teachers, administrators, and columnists who seem to believe that material should be hard for the sake of it and that education itself is best when rendered not in wonder but in force. I have never formally issued a "trigger warning" or explicitly carved out a "safe space." But I know that all readers do not come to a text equally. Some come surviving a rape, and some come caged in their assigned bodies, and some come having spent their entire young lives in classrooms with fellow students who made mascots of them. There seems to be an opportunity here, for comradeship, an invitation to allow for a more conversational literature, to revisit accepted ideas of voice and authority, to recognize that students are humans to be challenged, not animals to be broken and tamed.

It is very hard to challenge a student who arrives in class feeling endangered. This was always true of me.

When I applied to college, I applied to only one school that was not an HBCU, and that school was a fifteen-minute drive from my home. I would not have said it this way, if only because the language did not exist, but I needed to feel safe. I was living in an unsafe country, one whose culture and policies I hoped to someday write against. I needed to be surrounded by professors, students, and young writers who understood my mission—even if they didn't agree with it.

In my freshman year I took an Intro to Psychology class from Dr. Jules Harrell. I'd known him in a previous life, as "Baba Jules," a vindicationist and one of the men assembled to take me through my Rights of Passage when I was fourteen. Now, at Howard, I was forever stumbling in calling him "Baba" when I meant to say "Doctor." This confusion was made more difficult early in the semester when he announced that we would have a guest lecturer in our next session, Dr. William Shockley. I did not know who Dr. William Shockley was. Two days later, Dr. Harrell—or Baba Jules—walked into the classroom and promptly introduced himself as "Dr. Shockley." This was confusing enough, but then this "Dr. Shockley" proceeded to spend class presenting his argument, which held in sum that any gap between Black people and white people in test scores or life outcomes was because Black people were inherently less intelligent than white people. Class ended and we walked out, somewhat stunned by both the content and the device. But in our next session it was made clear that confusion was no excuse. It was a Monday. Dr. Harrell was himself again and before he went into the day's lecture he offered a firm directive: Don't you ever, in all your life, let someone say what I said to you on Friday and offer no response.

I think the self-appointed champions of free inquiry and debate would applaud that process—exposing a group of students to the devil's advocacy in the most confrontational manner. But, in fact, the entire exercise rested on a foundation of safety. I was at a Black university—surrounded by Black students and professors. Put differently, for me, the entire university was a "safe space." But how would I have felt, barely eighteen years old, being presented with this same case for my genetic inferiority by a white professor in a room full of white students? How would I feel knowing that some of those students—maybe even my professor—agreed with Shockley? What would the lesson have been? The fact is that I have been in "safe spaces" like Howard all my life, and they were essential for the necessary process of confronting a literature suffused with white supremacy. In childhood, there were wondrous comics and engrossing novels I read and was deeply influenced by, but these books were written by the disciples of racists like Edgar Rice Burroughs and Jules Verne. And then in college there was not just Shockley but Ezra Pound:

And you have been gone five months,
The monkeys make sorrowful noise overhead.

When I read that, I saw something in the shape and rhythm of words, and that something was transcendent and universal, no matter the author's affinity for Adolf Hitler. Even today, you can find me admiring Thomas Jefferson's elucidations on the evils of enslavement, all of them underwritten by those very evils themselves. And for much of my time as a journalist, I have been surrounded by people who, on some level, think of me as an exception that does not disprove their theories of white supremacy. Many of these people are themselves awful writers. But some of them are incredible—

and I have learned from them, and, as it happens, so have you.

And there's nothing high-minded about this. I don't really care much for hearing "both sides" or "opposing points of view," so much as I care about understanding the literary tools deployed to advance those views—the discipline of voice, the use of verbs, the length and brevity of sentences, and the curiosity of mind behind those sentences. It is this last I find so often lacking. Great canons angle toward great power, and the great privilege of great power is an incuriosity about those who lack it. That incuriosity is what afflicts the dullest critics of safe spaces and the like. But if these writers, teachers, and administrators could part with the privilege of their own ignorance, they would see that they too need safe spaces—and that, for their own sakes, they have made a safe space of nearly the entire world.

I've now taught in my fair share of different environments—prisons, libraries, public schools, and universities. My approach goes back to 1982. I am trying to entrance, to inspire, to excite, because I think that is exactly what I needed. But often plain human decency will suffice, and I've generally found that if I could explain to you why I was teaching Thomas Jefferson's thoughts on slavery, that if I granted you the right to hate him nonetheless if you so choose, and that if, most important of all, I made a general effort not to be an asshole, then you, in turn, tended to make a general effort to cope with all the requisite discomfort. My sense is that if I spend more time talking to you than I spend complaining about you, then something wonderful often happens and the enlightenment is mutual. So I don't really worry about the young, whose excesses are confined to lecture halls and quadrangles, so much as I fear the old, whose tyrannies are legislative.

The summer of 2020 now feels like distant history, and it is easy to be cynical about that season of protests given the backlash that followed. But I remember a different era, when the names of those killed died with the people who carried them. Those protests succeeded in implanting some skepticism in people who were raised on the idea of Officer Friendly. I think that is what the white supremacists feared most—the spreading realization that the cops were not knights and the creeping sense that there was something rotten not just in law enforcement but maybe also in the law itself. That fear explains the violent response to the protests, but even that violence redounded to the benefit of the protesters because it confirmed their critique. What was the justifiably noble interest that required tear-gassing protesters blocks from the Capitol, or the deployment of secret police in Portland, or the literal cracking of heads in Buffalo? White supremacists came to understand this, too, and though violence was never forsworn, by the end of the summer they had learned a lesson: The war might be raging in the streets, but it could never be defeated there, because what they were ultimately fighting was the word.

Around the same time George Floyd was killed, Nikole Hannah-Jones won a Pulitzer Prize for her lead essay in "The 1619 Project," which argued for America's origins not in the Declaration of Independence but in enslavement. Nikole is my homegirl, and like me, she believes that journalism, history, and literature have a place in our fight to make a better world. I had the great fortune of watching her build "The 1619 Project," of being on the receiving end of texts with highlighted pages from history books, of hearing her speak on the thrilling experience of telling our story, some four hundred years after we arrived here, in all the grandeur it deserved. Seeing the seriousness of effort, her passion for it, the platform she commanded, and the response it garnered, a backlash was certain to come. But I can't say I understood how profound this backlash would be— that a "1776 Project" would be initiated by the president, that the 2020 protests would be dubbed by some on the right as the "1619 Riots," thus explicitly, if in bad faith, connecting the writing and the street, and that the White House would issue Executive Order 13950, targeting any education or training that included the notion that America was "fundamentally racist," the idea that any race bore "responsibility for actions committed in the past," or any other "divisive concept" that should provoke "discomfort, guilt, anguish, or any other form of psychological distress on account of his or her race." It's true that the order was revoked after its author lost the next election, but by that time it had spawned a suite of state-level variants—laws, policies, directives, and resolutions—all erected to excise "divisive concepts" from any training or education. The flag of parental rights was raised. In Tennessee, teachers were fired. School boards in Virginia were besieged. And in North Carolina, Nikole's tenure offer from the state's flagship university—where she herself was an alum— was scotched at the behest of the Board of Trustees.

I guess it's worth pointing out the obvious—that the very governors and politicians who loudly exalt the values of free speech are among the most aggressive prosecutors of "divisive concepts." And I guess it should be noted that what these politicians—and even some writers—dubbed "critical race theory" bore little resemblance to that theory's actual study and practice. So I will note it. But the simple fact is that these people were liars, and to take them seriously, to press a case of hypocrisy or misreading, is to be distracted again. "The goal," as their most prominent activist helpfully explained, "is to have the public read something crazy in the newspaper and think 'critical race theory.'" It worked. Today, some four years after the signing of 13950, half the country's schoolchildren have been protected, by the state, from "critical race theory" and other "divisive concepts."

It may seem strange that a fight that began in the streets has now moved to the library, that a counterrevolution in defense of brutal policing has now transformed itself into a war over scholarship and art. But in the months after George Floyd's murder, books by Black authors on race and racism shot to the top of bestseller and most-borrowed lists. Black bookstores saw their sales skyrocket. The cause for this spike was, in the main, people who had been exposed to George Floyd's murder coming to suspect that they had not been taught the entire truth about justice, history, policing, racism, and any number of other related subjects. The spike only lasted that summer—but it was enough to leave the executors of 13950 shook. And they were right to be.

History is not inert but contains within it a story that implicates or justifies political order. So it was with Josiah Nott looking back to Ancient Egypt to justify slavery. And so it is with the American Revolution and the founding of a great republic, or the Greatest Generation who did not fight to defend merely the homeland but the entire world. If you believe that history, then you are primed to believe that the American state is a force for good, that it is the world's oldest democracy, and that those who hate America hate it for its freedoms. And if you believe that, then you can believe that these inexplicable haters of freedom are worthy of our drones. But a different history, one that finds its starting point in genocide and slavery, argues for a much darker present and the possibility that here too are haters of freedom, unworthy of the power they wield. A political order is premised not just on who can vote but on what they can vote for, which is to say on what can be imagined. And our political imagination is rooted in our history, our culture, and our myths. That the country's major magazines, newspapers, publishing houses, and social media were suddenly lending space to stories that questioned the agreed-upon narrative meant that Americans, as a whole, might begin to question them too. And a new narrative—and a new set of possibilities— might then be born.

Freire knew:

> The capability of banking education to minimize or annul the students' creative power and to stimulate their credulity serves the interests of the oppressors, who care neither to have the world revealed nor to see it transformed. The oppressors use their "humanitarianism" to preserve a profitable situation. Thus they react almost instinctively against any experiment in education which stimulates the critical faculties and is not content with a partial view of reality but always seeks out the ties which link one point to another and one problem to another.

It is very hard to be a writer from any community held outside of the promises of an order and be "content with a partial view of reality." It is impossible to write truthfully of Black people, in all our genius and folly, in all our joy and anguish, and not disturb those who "care neither to have the world revealed nor to see it transformed." So it was with Phillis Wheatley and Thomas Jefferson. So it is with Nikole Hannah-Jones and Donald Trump. In between Wheatley and Hannah-Jones, we are David Walker disappeared, Frederick Douglass brawling through the lecture circuit, Ida B. Wells run out of Memphis, and bookstores surveilled by the FBI. If American history really does begin in enslavement, in genocide, then the lies, and the policies that attack writing from beyond the order, must not just be deemed possible. They must be expected.

I wish I were better at that part—expecting. But the fact is that, even as I know and teach the power of writing, I still find myself in disbelief when I see that power at work in the real world. Maybe it is the nature of books. Film, music, the theater—all can be experienced amidst the whooping, clapping, and cheering of the crowd. But books work when no one else is looking, mind-melding author and audience, forging an imagined world that only the reader can see. Their power is so intimate, so insidious, that even its authors don't always comprehend it. I see politicians in Colorado, in Tennessee, in South Carolina moving against my own work, tossing books I've authored out of libraries, banning them from classes, and I feel snatched out of the present and dropped into an age of pitchforks and book-burning bonfires. My first instinct is to laugh, but then I remember that American history is filled with men and women who were as lethal as they were ridiculous. And when I force myself to take a serious look, I see something familiar: an attempt by adults to break the young minds entrusted to them and remake them in a more orderly and pliable form.

What these adults are ultimately seeking is not simply the reinstatement of their preferred dates and interpretations but the preservation of a whole manner of learning, austere and authoritarian, that privileges the apprehension of national dogmas over the questioning of them. The danger we present, as writers, is not that we will simply convince their children of a different dogma but that we will convince them that they have the power to form their own.

I know this directly. I imagine my books to be my children, each with its own profile and way of walking through the world. My eldest, *The Beautiful Struggle,* is the honorable, hardworking son. He has that union job my father once aspired to, four kids, and a wife he met in high school. My second son, *Between the World and Me,* is the "gifted" one, or rather the one whose gifts are most easily translated to the rest of the world. He plays in the NBA, enjoys the finer things, and talks more than he should. I see *We Were Eight Years in Power* as the insecure one, born in the shadow of my "gifted" son and who has never quite gotten over it. He has problems. We don't talk about him much. All these children suspect that my daughter, my baby girl, *The Water Dancer,* is my favorite. Perhaps. She certainly is the one that is most like me—if a little better, more confident, and more self-assured. I see my books this way because it helps me remember that though they are made by me, they are not ultimately mine. They leave home, travel, have their own relationships, and leave their own impressions. I've learned it's best to, as much as possible, stay out of the way and let them live their own lives.

My loyalty to that lesson is dispositional—I am often struck by secondhand embarrassment watching writers defend themselves against every bad review. But it's also strategic: My work is to set the table, craft the argument, render the world as I imagine it, and then go. The late

Jamal Khashoggi was fond of the Arabic proverb "Say your word, then leave." I try to live by that, because I am at my worst out there defending my children, and at my best making more of them.

But I began to see this kind of retreat into writing as a privilege. Out in the real world, teachers, parents, students, and librarians were under attack. They did not have the luxury of declining to defend themselves. I think a lot about this one note I received from Woodland Park, Colorado. The school board was trying to ban *Between the World and Me.* A parent wrote urging me to reach out to one of the teachers who was fighting the ban. "He believes in you and your message (as do I)," the parent wrote. "And he has been suffering for it." *Suffering.* It felt inhuman to let that pass. So I sent along a note of support. I even went on TV to call out the school board. But after that I retreated into my own private space of bookmaking.

And then I read about Mary Wood. The outlines of the case were not much different from others I'd heard: She was a teacher in South Carolina who had been forced to drop *Between the World and Me* from her lesson plan because it made some of her students, in their words, "feel uncomfortable" and "ashamed to be Caucasian." Moreover, they were sure that the very subject of the book—"systemic racism"—was "illegal." These complaints bore an incredible resemblance to the language of 13950, which prohibited "divisive concepts" that provoked in students "discomfort, guilt, anguish, or any other form of psychological distress on account of his or her race or sex." And it was not just the students' complaints that resembled the executive order— the South Carolina 2022 budget contained a prohibition lifted, nearly word for word, from 13950.

The connection between the legislation and 13950 was obvious. Still, for the first time I began to think about the vocabulary being employed—discomfort, shame, anguish—and how it read like a caricature of the vocabulary of safety that had become popular on campuses around the country. I suspect this was intentional. Oppressive power is preserved in the smoke and fog, and sometimes it is smuggled in the unexamined shadows of the language of the oppressed themselves. The strategy banks on the limited amount of time possessed by most readers and listeners and aims to communicate via shorthand that is just as often sleight of hand. It's not surprising that everyday people grappling with laundry, PTA meetings, and bills do not always see the device and the deception. But the difference is clear—Mary Wood's protesting students were not looking to attach a warning to *Between the World and Me* about its disturbing imagery or themes but to have the book, by force of law, removed from the state's school altogether.

Literature is anguish. Even small children know this. I was no older than five, crying in the back seat of my parents' orange Volkswagen while they argued up front. When they turned to comfort me, they were shocked to learn that I was crying not about their argument but about the grasshopper who starved in winter while the ant feasted. Thinking back, the Darryl Stingley story was an advance in an understanding that began the moment I could string sentences into stories. The wolf devours Grandma. The gingham dog and the calico cat devour each other. I was not born into a religious home, but I knew that my peers had been raised on stories of God casting Adam and Eve from paradise for biting an apple, that He had destroyed all life save that contained in the ark, that He had condemned me and every other nonbeliever to eternal suffering. And this is the children's literature of those who believe this to be a Christian nation. I suspect these believers would say that the anguish, this discomfort radiating out of their own gospel, is not incidental but is at the heart of its transformative power. For my part, the anguish of the grasshopper and the ant was in the moral of the story: that laziness and foolishness made one worthy of starvation. This kind of vengeance seemed unjust to me, and therein lay my personal revelation—one that apparently ran contrary to the story's intended message. But in my anguish, in my disagreement with the core of the text, I found my truth. And that, I suspect, is the real problem. Whatever the attempt to ape the language of college students, it was neither "anguish" nor "discomfort" that these people were trying to prohibit. It was enlightenment.

I tracked down Mary's number. We spoke for about half an hour. She talked about the whole ordeal—the paranoia incited by anonymous complaints; the school board meetings, where she was pilloried; the threats to her job. She spoke of the conservative tilt of the area where she taught, Chapin, South Carolina—a lakeside town to the northwest of the state capital of Columbia. She spoke of her own enlightenment, of going off to college and reading postcolonial literature until she felt the puzzle pieces of the world locking into place. She talked of George Floyd's murder and how she'd formed a book group with her department in that watershed summer. That was how she found *Between the World and Me.* We were the same age. We both had children who drove us crazy. We both practiced yoga for sanity. And she needed that practice now, more than ever. All this she said in an accent that told me that she was not just from someplace but of *that* someplace. And there was an affinity there, because I have an accent like that, and though acquired in another place still of that same remarkable genre. And there was something else just as remarkable. The section of Mary's class was not designed to expose her students to a certain set of politics but to show them the craft of writing an essay. Mary didn't teach civics or current events. She taught writing. Advanced Placement English, to be precise. For the exam, students would have to write an argumentative essay themselves, and to help them learn how, she'd called upon *Between the World and Me,* my loud and boisterous second son. Perhaps I am straining the metaphor, but I really did feel like one of my children had gone and gotten someone else into trouble.

"What will you do next year?" I asked Mary toward the end of our phone call.

"I'm going to finish the lesson I started," she said. "I'm going to teach *Between the World and Me.*"

I sat on the phone, silent, for eight seconds. Writing is all process to me, not finished work. It begins in the kind of anguish South Carolina sought to forbid, sometimes originating in something I've read, but more often in the world itself—in peoples and systems whose declared aims run contrary to their actions. And through reading, through reporting, I begin to comprehend a truth. That moment of comprehension is ecstatic. Writing and rewriting is the attempt to communicate not just a truth but the ecstasy of a truth. It is not enough for me to convince the reader of my argument; I want them to feel that same private joy that I feel alone. When I go out in the world, it's gratifying to hear that people have shared part of that joy, but Mary didn't just enjoy reading the book. The book had brought her into the fight.

I finally broke the silence. I told Mary that I had been thinking of coming down there, but I feared making a tense situation worse. But she urged me to come. There was a school board meeting in a week, which she and some of her supporters would attend.

By the next week I was with Mary, eating salad and drinking iced green tea at a restaurant in Chapin. She was the portrait of a familiar Southern archetype—blond, kind, outgoing, homegrown, daughter of the local football coach and a kindergarten teacher. Her claim to Chapin was strong—stronger even than some of the parents who despised her. The town had seen an influx of families looking to live somewhere conservative and traditional. Mary wasn't that. She was fighting for her job in the very school where she had earned her own high school diploma. How much this fact would help was unclear. Chapin High School was overseen by Lexington-Richland School District Five. The district has long tilted conservative. During the Trump years, it toppled. School board meetings were as much an open mic for reactionaries, conspiracy theorists, and attention-seekers as they were discussions of budgets and policies. The visible radicalization began with the district's response to Covid—local residents began queuing up at meetings to denounce masking mandates as tyranny and vaccination as "a violation of the Nuremberg Code." I've watched videos of these events, and the sources of the rage vented within them range. The rage went from masking and vaccination to DEI and pronouns. Something called "emotional learning" would catch an occasional stray. But mostly, the great enemy of Chapin was critical race theory. It was said that Lexington Five had become a staging ground for "educational warfare" on CRT, a doctrine that was held responsible for "anxiety, depression, and self-hatred," that raised suicide rates, and that made students "ashamed to be white." I was told that there was an occasional air of menace at the meetings, as when one speaker warned the board, "we are watching," or another claimed that the country was under the sway of practitioners of "pagan ways" and exponents of "child sacrifice" and the "drinking of blood." And it was quite normal for such sentiments to be applauded by spectators.

That Lexington Five school board meetings had become contentious was reflected in the security that greeted me at the door. I had to empty my pockets, permit my bag to be searched, and pass through a metal detector. On the other side I saw two beefy men dressed in army green with visible bulletproof vests. This struck me as a bad omen. But the guards greeted me politely, and when Mary and I turned the corner into the hallway leading to the meeting room, we were met by a woman named Brandi, a middle school science teacher. She stood in front of a table handing out flyers against censorship, and when she saw us, she smiled warmly.

Inside the meeting room, people milled around and chatted. There were tables at the front of the room, assembled in a U shape, with microphones and nameplates for the various officers of the district. We walked over to the side of the room opposite from the tables, where Mary's mother, Kathryn, waited for us. I shook her hand and her eyes grew big and she smiled. She pointed us to our seats, which she'd reserved, and in mine I found a copy of *Between the World and Me.*

"Would you sign, please?" Kathryn asked, still smiling.

I signed, sat down, and scanned the crowd. What I noticed was that half the people in the room were wearing blue T-shirts. Mary explained that blue was the district color, and Brandi had organized a group of sympathizers on Facebook, asking them to wear blue to show their support for Mary. An older woman named Bobbie sat next to me and we struck up a conversation. She did not know Mary and did not wear a blue T-shirt. But she explained that after George Floyd's death, her church had created a reading group around race. (She'd become a huge Colson Whitehead fan.) The head of that group read about Mary and urged all the members to come out and show support. This was the second time I'd heard of a reading group in this town as the epicenter of political disruption. From bell hooks on, books by Black authors helped Mary understand "why things are so fucked up." And it was these books that had brought Bobbie out to support Mary.

I understand the impulse to dismiss the import of the summer of 2020, to dismiss the "national conversations," the raft of TV specials and documentaries, even the protests themselves. Some of us see the lack of policy change and wonder if the movement itself was futile. But policy change is an end point, not an origin. The cradle of material change is in our imagination and ideas. And whereas white supremacy, like any other status quo, can default to the clichéd claims and excuses for the world as it is—bad cops are rotten apples, America is guardian of the free world—we have the burden of crafting new language and stories that allow people to imagine that new policies are possible. And now, even here in Chapin, some people, not most (it is hardly ever most), had, through the work of Black writers, begun that work of imagining.

The board chair gaveled the meeting to order at 7 P.M. sharp. She noted the full house and seemed to be girding herself for what was coming. The board called for a moment of silence for "a great tragedy," the specifics of which the chair did not explain. There was a prayer and the pledge of allegiance and a report from the superintendent on "academic freedom." From that point, allusions to Mary's case crept into the board's business until about an hour in, when, the undercard having been completed, the main event commenced. The board was giving the community its opportunity to speak.

As the first woman approached the microphone, I scanned the room, trying to ascertain the breadth of Mary's support. Only a few weeks earlier parents had queued up at this same monthly meeting to demand her firing. Now when I looked out I saw that the blue T-shirts were populous enough to indicate that her backers were deep. And then the comments began. It was a blowout. Parent after parent lined up to support Mary, most of them met by whooping cheers. A fourteen-year-old girl stood up and quoted from *Between the World and Me,* noting that in all her time in school she had never been assigned a book by a Black author. Mary cried silently and whispered to me a running commentary about each speaker—their family, their occupation, whether they had kids in the district. No one, not a single speaker, stood up to support the book's banning. I was initially surprised by this, but later I understood—school board meetings, and local politics, are small affairs, easily dominated by an organized faction, and that night the faction was Mary's.

Sometimes I will be at a reception or an event or even out on the street, and a brother will approach me to thank me for my work, and his build, how he moves, his language, his haircut will inform me that he has just finished a bid. I see these brothers and I remember my time teaching at Lorton. I see these brothers and I see that shadow version of myself that my parents and teachers warned would take shape if the notes in lipstick red continued, if my "conduct" did not improve. The line between us feels thin. And perhaps for that reason, I feel a warmth from them too, very similar to what I felt in Dakar, very similar to what I feel with you, because we are all laboring under the shadow. There was not a single person like that in the audience at that hearing, which was about what I expected. And I'd spoken to enough audiences to understand that if you're lucky your writing moves beyond your imagined circle, and then you feel another warmth, different, broader, but warmth all the same. But I wasn't speaking here. I wasn't even the subject. What I seemed to be witnessing was as much about a book as it was something more localized— a kind of referendum on the school district's identity.

Mary taught an advanced placement class, which is to say her audience was not kids meandering off to college, as I had, but students aiming for college credits and a head start in that world. There was a sense in the room that avoiding "divisive concepts" was not just wrong on moral grounds but that it represented a lowering of standards; that to ban a book was to erect a kind of South Carolina exception for advanced placement—one that validated the worst caricatures of Southern whiteness often bandied by the kind of Northerner who thinks "we should have just let them secede." The room was embarrassed. I remember one man, Josh Gray, a professor of math at the University of South Carolina, standing up, his hair pulled back in a ponytail, and bringing this self-inflicted humiliation into view in a way that would never have occurred to me. "I can tell you, as a redneck who's worked all over the world and met people from all over the world," he said, "don't make the perception that [the students] have to compete against worse by actions like this that do not reflect well on our community."

This may seem self-interested, a stance taken more to avoid a stigma than to break an arrangement of power. Given the kind of loud virtue signaling that followed 2020, I understand the question. But virtues *should* be signaled, and the signalers should act to make their virtues manifest. It is the latter, not the former, that is the problem. And I doubt that anyone ever parts with power in the name of charity. In this case, self-interest meant that here in the heart of Jim Crow and Redemption, ideas to the contrary could not be driven from the public square. And that is progress. It just isn't inevitable that such progress continues.

The following afternoon, I met Mary for barbecue. I was actually giddy from the night before. I had expected to come into a den of hectoring fanatics. And instead I'd found that there were allies fighting back. *Allies.* When I started writing, it felt essential to think of white people as readers as little as possible, to reduce them in my mind, to resist the temptation to translate. I think that was correct. What has been surprising—pleasantly so— is that there really is no translation needed, that going deeper actually reveals the human. Get to the general through the specific, as the rule goes. Still, even as I have come to understand this, it feels abstract to me. What I wanted was to be Mary for a moment, to understand how she came to believe that it was worth risking her job over a book.

Mary's grandfather was a social worker and World War II vet who was blinded disarming mines. He came home a ferocious advocate for the disabled, but Black disabled veterans particularly. Although Mary knew her grandfather, he didn't talk about his history as an activist. She found out from a book after his death. Her parents were more liberal than the norm—the type who in a red voting district still put out a Biden 2020 lawn sign. But what she mostly had growing up was an ill-defined sense that the world, as it was conventionally explained, didn't make sense. She'd been bred to be a Southern lady, but it didn't really take. She had to be bribed into etiquette class with Bojangles. In church, Mary did not obsess over being saved so much as she wondered why there were no women in the pulpit. And then in college, books righted the frame: She read bell hooks's *Talking Back: Thinking Feminist, Thinking Black.* When she finished, she called her mother and said, "This is why things are so fucked up."

It was exactly the experience that the purveyors of 13950, the book banners, and those targeting CRT were seeking to prevent. We finished eating and took a drive over to the state capitol. South Carolina was the first state to secede and also the state where both Reconstruction and Redemption reached their most spectacular ends. All through that period, South Carolina had been a majority-Black state, and at the height of Reconstruction, before its undoing in Redemption, the state was home to an emancipated working class and a multiracial democracy. It's quite the story—but it's not the one that the State House tells. There is a beautiful sculpture there wrought by the astronaut turned artist Ed Dwight. But most of the sprawling twenty-two acres of the State House proper are a shrine to white supremacy. A collection of giant statues sits on raised platforms, so that men like Strom Thurmond, who pinned his entire political career on segregation, loom like gods. Wade Hampton, who enslaved generations and then fought in a bloody war to uphold that system, is there. So is Ben Tillman, who once boasted of lynching from the Senate floor. He knew of what he spoke. In 1876, Tillman pitched in to massacre Black people in Hamburg, and in 1895, he'd rallied white South Carolinians to write Black people out of the state's constitution. The movement to erase Black people from politics swept through the South and won the day in legislatures, state houses, and courts. But if you just looked at the obvious organs of the government, you'd miss the breadth of the attack.

Recounting the exploitation of the peasants of medieval Europe, the historian Barbara Tuchman wrote in *A Distant Mirror* that in the "tales and ballads" of the time, peasants were depicted as "aggressive, insolent, greedy, sullen, suspicious, tricky, unshaved, unwashed, ugly, stupid." Tuchman quotes from stories of the time asserting that an unexploited peasantry "troubles God," and the universe can only be set right when peasants are left to "eat thistles and briars, thorns and straw." The stories justified the forced labor of feudalism—emphasis on "forced":

> The records tell of peasants crucified, roasted, dragged behind horses by the brigands to extort money. There were preachers who pointed out that the peasant worked unceasingly for all, often overwhelmed by his tasks, and who pleaded for more kindness, but all they could advise the victim was patience, obedience, and resignation.

I remember reading this and being shocked by how familiar it all was, right down to the notion of better luck in the next life. But I shouldn't have been shocked. The narratives about serfs—the Niggerology of thirteenth-century Europe—justified their exploitation. And this was as true during the Middle Ages as it was during Jim Crow. You don't raise the kind of looming statues I saw at the State House just for the hell of it. Politics is the art of the possible, but art creates the possible of politics. A policy of welfare reform exists downstream from the myth of the welfare queen. Novels, memoirs, paintings, sculptures, statues, monuments, films, miniseries, advertisements, and journalism all order our reality. Jim Crow segregation—with its signage and cap-doffing rituals—was both policy and a kind of public theater. The arts tell us what is possible and what is not, because, among other things, they tell us who is human and who is not. All the Gold Dust Twins and Korn Kinks, all the Sambos and Niggerheads, all the spooks and coons, all the Uncle Bens and Aunt Jemimas, all the Nigger-Dies-First and Black-Bitch-Craves-Dick are, at their core, the founding myths of an empire.

And they wrote this down. In the nineteenth century, as ex-slaves sought to build the first egalitarian democracy in American history, they were opposed by white men who claimed to be "Redeemers"—not just of government and society but of history and art. They raised statues. They wrote histories, memoirs, and novels. And then, with the work of Redemption complete, more stories were published so that terrorists and bandits would be remembered as knights and champions. Jesse James is America's own Robin Hood, an outlaw hailed in novels, film, and music for standing against the great forces of industrial capitalism, the railroads, and the robber barons of the North. Art hides the truth of Jesse James—that he was the scion of a slaveholding family, that he fought on the side of slavery and then against Reconstruction, and that in his first train robbery he wore a Ku Klux Klan mask. In time, even that symbol of terrorism would itself be redeemed.

When D. W. Griffith wanted to "shoot a large arrow right into the heart of American cinema," he knew exactly what story to tell, and he knew exactly how to do it, and it would not be art for art's sake. The Civil War "hasn't been told accurately in history books," Griffith asserted. "Only the winning side in the war ever gets to tell its story." This was an exaggeration, the kind of inversion that power uses to justify itself—the way the bully pretends to be the victim to add virtue to his violence. But the "losers" of the Civil War were not victims. In fact, *Birth of a Nation* shared its worldview with the president of the United States, Woodrow Wilson. Griffith used texts from Woodrow Wilson's ten-volume *History of the American People* throughout the film. In turn, Wilson screened the film at the White House. This was art as politics, and it was monstrously successful. It remade the business of cinema, the art of film, and American history. Inspired by *Birth of a Nation,* the second Ku Klux Klan was born, taking their rituals—which haunt us to this day—directly from the film. And then in 1919, four years after the film's premiere, the Red Summer and the scourge of lynching swept the country. Life imitated art, and Black people were left fleeing and fighting for their lives.

We have lived under a class of people who ruled American culture with a flaming cross for so long that we regularly cease to notice the import of being ruled at all. But they do not. And so the Redeemers of this age look out and see their kingdom besieged by trans Barbies, Muslim mutants, daughters dating daughters, sons trick-or-treating as Wakandan kings. The fear instilled by this rising culture is not for what it does today but what it augurs for tomorrow—a different world in which the boundaries of humanity are not so easily drawn and enforced. In this context, the Mom for Liberty shrieking "Think of the children!" must be taken seriously. What she is saying is that her right to the America she knows, her right to the biggest and greenest of lawns, to the most hulking and sturdiest SUVs, to an arsenal of infinite AR-15s, rests on a hierarchy, on an order, helpfully explained and sanctified by her country's ideas, art, and methods of education.

That is the heart of it. It is not a mistake that Mary

teaches writing at its most advanced level and has found herself a target. Much of the current hoopla about "book bans" and "censorship" gets it wrong. This is not about me or any writer of the moment. It is about writers to come—the boundaries of their imagination, the angle of their thinking, the depth of their questions. I can't say I knew it, that first day walking into Lorton, but in my time teaching it soon became clear that becoming a good writer would not be enough. We needed more writers, and I had a responsibility to help them as a reader, to be an active audience for the stories they wanted to tell, or as a teacher, so that they could learn to tell them better, to reach deeper into their own truth in the same way that brought me euphoria, and reach into the hearts of readers and set them on fire, as Mary had been set on fire since college: by words on a page.

As we walked the grounds of the State House, I thought about what it meant for a young student to visit these same grounds. I thought about what it must mean to walk amongst these Klansmen, enslavers, and segregationists raised up on their platforms to the status of titans. I thought about what it means to go back to the schools, where work questioning this beatification is slowly being pushed out, to the libraries that are being bleached of discomforting stories. And I thought how it all works not simply to misinform but to miseducate; not just to assure the right answers are memorized but that the wrong questions are never asked. And I thought about myself back in Baltimore and what I was being trained for. I was saved by the books in my house, by the implicit message that learning does not belong exclusively in schools. Who would I be, left to the devices of those who seek to shrink education, to make it orderly and pliable? I don't know. But I know what I would not be: a writer.

The statues and pageantry can fool you. They look like symbols of wars long settled, fought on behalf of men long dead. But their Redemption is not about honoring a past. It's about killing a future.

IV.

———◆ ◆———

The Gigantic Dream

We have all been lied to about too much.

NOURA ERAKAT

On the last day of my trip to Palestine, I visited Yad Vashem, the World Holocaust Remembrance Center. I don't know that I've ever seen a more striking site of mourning. It was late May, when the weather in the Levant is dry and warm. Here, as at Gorée, I refused the guided tour, preferring to wander this complex—its buildings, monuments, and landscaped grounds—in the company of my own impressions. I began by walking into a large building with ivory walls, where I found myself facing the massive Book of Names—seventy separate tomes stretching almost the entire length of the eight-meter-long hall that contains it, holding some 17,500 pages, each the height of an adult human being, and on those pages are the names of nearly five million Jews who were murdered in the Holocaust.

I slowly rounded the length of the Book, thumbing through the pages, pausing from time to time, until I had circumnavigated the entire cataclysm. I was barely twenty minutes into my visit, and already I felt the need to rest. I sat down on a nearby bench, falling into a kind of thoughtless reflection, wherein I felt but did not speak—even to myself. The human mind can only conceive of so much tragedy at once—and when lost lives spiral into the hundreds, then thousands, and then millions, when murder becomes a wide, seemingly unending mass, we lose our ability to see its victims as anything more than an abstract, almost theoretical, collection of lives. In this way, a second crime is perpetrated: Human beings are reduced to a gruel of misery. At Yad Vashem, the sheer enormity of the book mirrors the breadth of the crime it records, but the names, each one clearly inscribed, stand out against the mass of the thing, like stars dotting the night. In this sense, the Book of Names does exactly what we writers seek to do. It clarifies.

I sat on the bench watching as a young couple, speaking French to each other, flipped through the Book searching for the name of a lost relative. Then I stood up and left that ivory-walled room and walked down the Avenue of the Righteous Among the Nations, a long outdoor space dedicated to those gentiles who risked their lives on behalf of the Jews hunted by Hitler. At the end of the Avenue, I entered Yad Vashem's Holocaust History Museum. I've walked the spiraling halls of the National Museum of African-American History, a journey that begins in the depths of a slave ship. I've been to the Whitney Plantation in New Orleans, which does not center itself on Southern belles and mint juleps but on the system of forced labor that bound, worked, and whipped human beings within an inch of their lives and beyond. I've stood before the earthworks at the Wilderness in Virginia, where men were burned alive in a war to uphold that same system. That America gives more attention to the genocides abroad than to the genocides at home might fool you into a quasi-denialism, where you might think the Holocaust's evils are exaggerated for effect. This is wrong. Every time I visit a space of memory dedicated to this particular catastrophe, what I always come away thinking is that it was worse than I thought, worse than I could ever imagine. And Yad Vashem was no exception.

I entered the main building and confronted a collage of home movies taken in the years when that technology was still new. Fragmented footage of Jewish communities were stitched together so that they appeared to be a single rolling piece of film. I was too stunned to take notes on all the images, but one image still haunts—two little girls facing the camera, waving, beckoning me across the years. Then they disappeared, and I felt myself standing on the conveyor belt of time, moving through a world that too was about to be disappeared.

I walked on, slowly making my way through the museum. I saw the portraits of murdered families. I saw the braided whips used to drive Jewish captives to work in the camps. There was a map with captions and bar graphs laying bare the awful percentages—3 million of 3.25 million Polish Jews wiped out. And there were moments of great heroism—one exhibit told the story of the fifty thousand Jews saved by Dimitar Peshev, the deputy speaker of the Bulgarian Parliament. I felt guilty for needing these rare moments of narrative relief, if only because writing has taught me the virtue of facing horror with no demand for a cheap and easy hope. But when you stand there and behold the story of the Klooga concentration camp, whose Nazi masters were so set on murder that they killed some two thousand Jews rather than see them rescued by the Russian troops who were mere days away, you begin to feel hope itself slipping through your fingers, and not just hope for the Jewish captives in Klooga. In a place like this, your mind expands as the dark end of your imagination blooms, and you wonder if human depravity has any bottom at all, and if it does not, what hope is there for any of us?

But it had been that kind of trip—an expansion of the darkness, a grappling with its size, its shape, its weight. I remember standing before an exhibit telling the story of the *Struma,* a rickety vessel that carried some 781 Jews out of certain death in Romania to the borders of Turkey. Its passengers pled for entry to Mandatory Palestine, then under British rule. The refugees were refused, towed out through the Bosporus Strait into the Black Sea, and abandoned. The next day an errant Russian torpedo struck the ship. Everyone was killed except nineteen-year-old David Stoliar. Here was a man who knew the darkness well. He'd been expelled from school in Romania for the crime of being Jewish and then done a stint in a labor camp, all before he'd even boarded the *Struma.* And by 1948, Stoliar was free, a soldier fighting to draw a Jewish state out of the Zionist imagination and into the real.

Israel's formation, the light out of the Shoah's darkness, has long been held up as an uplifting coda to the Holocaust, an exemplar of the long arc of the moral universe bending toward justice. I saw the connection made right there at Yad Vashem in one of its last exhibits: a black-and-white reel of David Ben-Gurion declaring the creation of the Israeli state. This arc—from Holocaust to nation-state—has been traced in film, literature, and global memory. The relentless grimness of *Schindler's List* finds its relief in the unwanted, wandering Jews, saved by Schindler, finding a home in their Promised Land while "Jerusalem of Gold" plays in the background. In this way the want of relief can be permanently sated: Two thousand years of wrong has at last been righted, and a people, persecuted, hunted, and subjected to industrialized genocide, has not only survived but found its way back to a God-given home.

Home—with all its implications of safety, warmth, and family—is only half of Israel's national story. It is not just that the Jewish people were finally left to cultivate their own Promised Land, free from the terror of gentiles, but that upon that Promised Land they erected a Jewish state, which is to say the Jewish nation cleaved to an official Jewish flag, an official Jewish language, and an official Jewish army. And what that meant was not just freedom but power. After mass murder in the Rhineland, after all civilization had abandoned them to the gas chambers, after Dreyfus and Shylock, after expulsion from Spain, after two thousand years of depredations, the Jewish people had taken their place among The Strong. The shape of this story is not just the curving arc of justice but something more: a perfect circle. Not merely a righting but a restoration, a redemption.

And this redemption was evident the moment I entered Yad Vashem, because the first thing I saw there was not an exhibit but a row of twenty-odd soldiers in fatigues, carrying guns the size of small children. And they were almost children themselves—barely out of high school, by their appearance—and engaged in some kind of banter known only to them. I stood there staring, probably longer than I should have. There was something incongruous about so many guns being so flagrantly wielded in so solemn a place. I knew that they were there to protect this site from those who would wish Hitler's work more complete. But by then, I knew that that was not all the soldiers of this country were protecting.

On my first full day in Jerusalem, I walked with a group of fellow writers, editors, and artists into the Old City of Jerusalem. We were staying in East Jerusalem, which has been under Israeli occupation, along with the West Bank and Gaza, since 1967. There were about a dozen of us total, pulled from all over the world—South

Africa, Kashmir, the U.K., and America—at the invitation of the Palestine Festival of Literature. For five days our hosts took us from city to city so that we might see Palestine from the ground. The sun hung big and brilliant in a cloudless open sky, but the air was relatively cool. Our group of companions walked to the brink of the Lion's Gate, where we met the custodian of one of Islam's holiest sites: the Al-Aqsa complex, which includes the Al-Aqsa Mosque and the Dome of the Rock. This was the object of our visit, but it was made difficult by the phalanx of soldiers who examined our passports and then, for no discernible reason, made us wait.

The land of the Al-Aqsa complex is holy to both Muslims and Jews. Muslims believe that Al-Aqsa is where the prophet Muhammad ascended to heaven. The Jewish people have a different name for the Al-Aqsa complex: the Temple Mount, hallowed ground that derives its power from an alloy of collective legend, collective biography, and historical fact. All three Abrahamic religions—Christianity, Judaism, and Islam—believe Temple Mount to be the site of a temple built by the biblical King Solomon. Beyond faith, Temple Mount is also the site of King Herod's Temple. And while archaeological evidence for Solomon's temple is scant, the existence of King Herod's Temple is settled fact. And then there is prophecy, for it is held by some avid believers that a third temple will someday be erected at Temple Mount, thus heralding the coming of the Messiah. The Western Wall at the edge of Al-Aqsa is all that remains of Herod's temple and is also the area allotted for Jews to worship under an agreement called the "status quo," which divides the Old City into separate worship zones for Jews, Christians, and Muslims. Modern Jerusalem itself is divided between East and West, the former mostly populated by Palestinians and the latter by Israelis. Advocates of a two-state solution have long imagined West Jerusalem as the capital of Israel and East Jerusalem as the capital of the Palestinian state. The Old City is in East Jerusalem, and, for the moment, a Jordanian-funded Waqf exercises nominal control of Al-Aqsa. But the real control belongs to the occupying power, with predictable results: Israelis regularly tour Al-Aqsa, while Palestinians are barred from the Western Wall.

We stood at the Lion's Gate for the next forty-five minutes or so, talking amongst ourselves, unsure of what was happening or why we had been stopped. Was it that we had cameras? Was it that our guide was Jordanian? No justifications were given, no questions asked, no instructions offered. The soldiers just stood there with their enormous guns, blocking the way. I leaned against a nearby wall and watched as groups of tourists streamed in and out of the Gate, unmolested and unquestioned. But no one visibly Muslim passed through the Lion's Gate in all the time we were made to wait. I could not quite put words to what I was seeing, but watching those soldiers stand there and steal our time, the sun glinting off their shades like Georgia sheriffs, I could feel the lens of my mind curving to refract the blur of new and strange events.

The next day, I was with this same group, walking through the old city of Hebron with Walid Abu al-Halawah, a local urbanist. Al-Halawah, in tinted glasses, dark jeans, and a long-sleeve green shirt, explained that when he was a child, this city had been open and bustling, with a thriving market and streams of pilgrims coming to visit Al-Haram Al-Ibrahimi, which is traditionally believed to be the burial ground of Abraham, Sarah, Isaac, and Jacob. But as in the Old City, Israeli soldiers exercised total control over all movement through the town. We were standing at the gate to Al-Shuhada Street, which was once the main market street of Old Hebron. Palestinians are now barred from Al-Shuhada Street, while settlers move as they please through the whole town. "There are 126 Israeli cameras filming and recording the whole way here," Walid said. Then he pointed toward rooftop after rooftop and said, "There is a camera there. A camera over there. A camera there."

The city's most visible feature was its amazing variety of checkpoints—some of them were just soldiers lingering around, others massive gates with metal turnstiles. As we approached one, I watched two Palestinian schoolchildren being stopped by a soldier and directed back down the street from which they had come. And then it was our turn. One by one we approached. They checked our passports and allowed us to proceed. These soldiers roam as they feel, stopping and interrogating according to their whim. Later that day, I walked out to buy some goods from a shopkeeper. But before I could get there, a soldier walked out from a checkpoint, blocked my path, and asked me to state my religion. He looked at me skeptically when I told him I did not have one and asked for my parents' religion. When I told him they were not religious either, he rolled his eyes and asked about my grandparents. When I told him they were Christian, he allowed me to pass.

If this had happened in America, I would have told you that the soldier who stopped me was Black, and I guess he was here too. In fact, there were "Black" soldiers everywhere lording their power over the Palestinians, many of whom would, in America, have been seen as "white." Again I felt the mental lens curving against the light and was reminded of something I have long known, something I've written and spoken about, but still was stunned to see here in such stark detail: that race is a species of power and nothing else. And I knew here, in this moment, how I would have fallen in the hierarchy of power if I had told that Black soldier that I was a Muslim. And on that street so far from home, I suddenly felt that I had traveled through time as much as through space.

For as sure as my ancestors were born into a country where none of them was the equal of any white man, Israel was revealing itself to be a country where no Palestinian is ever the equal of any Jewish person anywhere. This fact is not hard to discern. Beyond my own initial impressions, there is the law itself, which clearly and directly calls for a two-tier society. Jewish citizens of Israel who marry Christians from Scotland can pass their citizenship on to their spouse and children; Palestinian citizens of Israel cannot. Jewish Israelis in Jerusalem are citizens of the state; Palestinians in the city are merely "permanent residents," a kind of sub-citizenship with a reduced set of rights and privileges. In Hebron,

Jewish settlers are subject to civil law, with all its rights and protections, while stateless Palestinians in the same city are subject to military courts, with all their summary power and skepticism.

The separate and unequal nature of Israeli rule is both intense and omnipresent—something I saw directly. The roads and highways we traveled were marked off for license plates of different colors—yellow, used mostly by those who are Jewish, and white with green lettering, used almost entirely by those who are not. As we drove these roads along the West Bank, our guide pointed out settlements—a word that I had always taken to refer to rugged camps staked out in the desert but in fact the settlements are more akin to American subdivisions, distinguished from the villages of the Palestinians by homes with large red roofs, as surely as a white picket fence denoted the suburbs of twentieth-century America and not its teeming cities.

On many of the Palestinian roofs I saw large cisterns for the harvesting of rainwater. These cisterns were almost certainly illegal—the Israeli state's hold on the West Bank includes control of the aquifers in the ground and the rainwater that falls from above. Any structure designed for gathering water requires a permit from the occupying power, and such permits are rarely given to

Palestinians. The upshot is predictable—water consumption for Israelis is nearly four times that of Palestinians living under occupation. And in those West Bank settlements which I once took as mere outposts, you can find country clubs furnished with large swimming pools. On seeing these cisterns, it occurred to me that Israel had advanced beyond the Jim Crow South and segregated not just the pools and fountains but the water itself. And more, it occurred to me that there was still one place on the planet—under American patronage—that resembled the world that my parents were born into.

And I was in that world, even as I walked haltingly through Yad Vashem, which is, among other things, a grand narrative of conquered ancestors built by their conquering progeny. I can see that, now that I have walked the land. But there was a time when I took my survey from afar, and invoked this same land to service my own, more narrow story. It hurts to tell you this. It hurts to know that in my own writing I have done to people that which, in this writing, I have inveighed against—that I have reduced people, diminished people, erased people. I want to tell you I was wrong. I want to tell you that your oppression will not save you, that being a victim will not enlighten you, that it can just as easily deceive you. I learned that here. In Haifa. In Ramallah. And especially here at Yad Vashem. So this is another story about writing, about power, about settling accounts, a story not of redemption but of reparation.

When I think of my earliest days as a writer, what I recall is a kind of longing—I *felt* everything I wished to say, even if I didn't exactly *know* it. There was so much I did not understand, and what I did understand I could never say with all the layers and color that would truly convey that understanding to my reader. I would fall in love with some girl and find my emotions so dominated that the only vent I had was writing it down. But when I pulled out my black-and-white composition notebook and put pen to paper, what I saw instead were the words of a thousand other men who had gone before me. I had no voice, which is to say no cadence, no lexicon, no sense of beauty I could call my own. I would stay up late reading Etheridge Knight's "As You Leave Me," over and over wondering how the hell he did it. What does it mean to watch a woman you love "disappear in the dark streets/to whistle and smile at the johns"? I was so young. I knew what it was to want one way and to be wanted in another—but not like this, not with a woman who went out "to whistle and smile at the johns." That phrase was such an elegant description of sex work that I think that even if Etheridge Knight himself had never had that experience, he knew enough about the life to make us feel like he had. There was a lesson for me in that. I know there are writers who can imagine a world from nothing. But I'm not one of them. The sense of beauty I was seeking had to emerge from knowledge.

Ten years ago, I acquired the sense that all of the skills and techniques I have discussed with you—the beauty inherent in the feel and rhythm of words, the great import of direct reporting and deep research, the force of active and intentional language, the power of tense, the gravity of history—was at last in my clutches. I did not think myself a master of this entire arsenal, but I felt that I well understood its uses. And more, I had, shockingly to me, found myself writing for *The Atlantic*—a storied magazine, with the resources to gird and strengthen my writing. This was crucial. I trace myself back to a line of autodidact writers, men and women who felt themselves in possession of some essential truth but were forced to testify to that truth without fact checkers, copy editors, and access to distant archives and expensive databases to perfect that testimony. But I now had those tools, and I understood that whatever power I now felt I possessed as a writer, the amplifying power of the institution around me was indispensable.

All this I brought to bear, at length, in an essay for *The Atlantic,* "The Case for Reparations." As I wrote, I could feel it flowing through me—all the study of language, all the reading, all the reporting—all of it coming together in what felt to me like a dissertation with an audience of one. That sounds crazy, I know. But in the months before the article was published, I felt that I had at last discovered the answer to the haunting question of why my people so reliably settled at the bottom of nearly every socioeconomic indicator. The answer was simple: The persistence of our want was matched exactly to the persistence of our plunder. I was blessed with a gift, and the gift was not simply the knowledge that "they" were lying (about us, about this country, and about themselves) but the proof—studies, monographs, and my own reporting. And I had an institution that vouched for the validity of this exercise, which put its weight and clout behind it. I guess it's odd for me, who preaches the power of writing, to tell you this, but I was shocked by everything that came of that union. I had set my sights relatively low—to synthesize the scholarship and journalism in some dynamic and gripping fashion, to "make political writing into an art," as Orwell had implored, so that the idea of reparations, the notion that we had been robbed and must be repaid, would no longer be so easily laughed at by the robbers. Maybe that was my mistake.

Making a charge according to the law of those you indict is a dangerous business. However much you try to remember your own motives, however much you may feel yourself to have succeeded, you are ultimately in their world and are thus compelled to speak to them through their symbols and stories. The need is even greater when you are a stranger to them, an adversary even, because your claims are always viewed with more skepticism. I lived in a world of white editors and white writers. I respected and admired many of them professionally and considered some of them friends. This was mutual, and there were very few places that I felt were more open to my resourcing and cultivating my writing and imagination than *The Atlantic*. I think now I felt grateful even to have the chance to publish what I considered so radical a proposition on the cover of such a hallowed and lauded magazine. But I also felt that I was attempting to display the truth and gravity of the debt of white supremacy for people who did not understand intuitively, and who would have great difficulty ever imagining that debt being repaid. And so to make the case, I reached for the same story invoked by Yad Vashem—the perfect circle, from Holocaust to state— and Germany's efforts to pay off its own inconceivable debt by making reparations to the state of Israel.

I had then a vague notion of Israel as a country that was doing something deeply unfair to the Palestinian people, though I was not clear on exactly what. And I knew there was a long history of alliances between Palestinian freedom fighters and the radical Black activists to whom I traced my own roots. I remember watching *World News Tonight* with my father, and deriving from him a dull sense that the Israelis were "white" and the Palestinians were "Black," which is to say that the former were the oppressors and the latter the oppressed. And once—back when I dreamed of being a poet— my father had handed me a book by the Palestinian-American poet Suheir Hammad titled *Born Palestinian, Born Black,* and this combination felt natural to me, though I could not have then articulated why.

What I had was a human instinct that a grave injustice was being imposed on the Palestinians, one that likely dates back to the vindicationist skepticism of America and what I perceived as whiteness. But I became a journalist just at the moment that I began to feel both vindicationism and a politics of instinct as incomplete. So I was proud of "The Case for Reparations" because it did rely on instinct but was a synthesis of facts. It was crafted in the mold of the (mostly white) magazine writers I'd admired. They were courageous reporters and masters at taking in many streams of that reporting and turning it into a coherent and gripping narrative. Quite a few of them wrote about the "Israeli-Palestinian conflict," and from their writing I derived a sense that comprehension of "conflict" was a matter of knowledge, not morality. And that knowledge was as foreign to me as computational mathematics. To that was added my steady diet of beat reports, Sunday talk shows, and loose conversation, all of which validated the apparent complexity over the "conflict." But even amid that complexity there was a certain incontestable narrative punctuated by platitudes that assumed an air of indisputable truth: Israel was a "Jewish democracy," indeed "the only democracy in the Middle East," one with both "the right to exist" and "the right to defend itself."

I had staked my writing largely against exactly these sorts of easy bromides and national fictions. And I'd been richly rewarded and well honored for that work. But the year I wrote "The Case for Reparations" was the same year I applied for my first adult passport. My

work was as local as it was lauded—and somewhere in
my mind, I was still a college dropout, still "Ta-Nehisi
was restless today" written in lipstick red. I felt the great
hand of luck in my life, and I was now, miraculously,
surrounded by people who knew real things about the
world—journalists who had covered civil wars and had
been evacuated from war zones and knew the correct
use of words like "internecine" and "sectarian." I felt my
deep ignorance of the world beyond America's borders
and, with that, a deep shame.

But passport stamps and wide vocabularies are neither wisdom nor morality. As it happens, you can see
the world and still never see the people in it. Empires are
founded by travelers, and the claim of some exclusive
knowledge of the native is their mark. I always imagined
reparations as a rejection of plunder at large. And who
in modern memory had been plundered more than the
victims of the Holocaust? But my prototype was not
reparations from a genocidal empire to its Jewish victims, but from that empire to a Jewish state. And what
my young eyes now saw of that state was a world where
separate and unequal was alive and well, where rule by
the ballot for some and the bullet for others was policy.
I was seeking a world beyond plunder—but my proof of
concept was just more plunder.

Halfway through my trip, I joined my group of writers for a hike up to the top of a hill just outside of Ramallah. The sun blazed above while briars attacked from below. But whatever the assault of nature, I was relieved to feel myself beyond the walls, strictures, and devices of humans. Our destination was Sakiya—an ecological retreat where a collective of Palestinians were reimagining their relationship with this precious land, which certain forces seemed determined to rip right out from under them. And it is precious—two of the houses here are from the Ottoman period and the British mandate, respectively, and there is a shrine dating back to the twelfth century. In 1937, the site was purchased from a farming family by Daoud Zalatimo, the Palestinian artist and educator. Zalatimo would host his family here for three months in the summer, and drew inspiration from the site's vistas. In one of his paintings, his young son, Ibrahim, is seated in a red toy car, looking out placidly, a verdant garden blooming in the background. Contemplating this work, the art historian John Halaka wondered, "Why does this unassuming painting feel like a ghost haunting me?" In 1948, as Palestinians were being driven from their land, Zalatimo sheltered his family on his estate. And then, in 1967, Zalatimo too was driven out by Israeli forces. He and his family were banned from returning, except for day visits. Zalatimo died in 2001.

Our guide through the history and landscape of the site was Sahar Qawasmi, the architect and co-founder of Sakiya, with her partner, the filmmaker Nida Sinnokrot. Sahar was born in Kuwait, but her family is from Palestine—Ramallah, Hebron, Jordan. During the Second Intifada, as Palestinians battled Israeli occupation and cities like Hebron became combat zones, the Israeli Defense Forces expanded its network of checkpoints and enforced a curfew. Feeling imprisoned, Sahar, then a student at nearby Birzeit University, began exploring the hills around Ramallah with friends. During one of these walks, Sahar found the Zalatimo estate, which had not been lived in since 1967, though the property was still in the family. There was trash everywhere. Vandals had ripped up the property in search of valuables. Nature had taken over and there were trees growing through the floors. Nonetheless, there was "a magic about it," Sahar told me later. Maybe it was the house built on the hill overlooking a valley. Maybe it was that the site couldn't be reached by car, and every journey had the feel of a pilgrimage. Maybe it was the sheer vintage of the site—archaeological evidence dates back through the time of the Crusaders, the Romans, and the Canaanites. Or maybe it was the water—a natural spring still in its traditional form. Whatever it was, it left Sahar with a feeling of "holiness." She and Nida founded Sakiya in 2016 and they have been trying to preserve that holiness ever since.

The effort was constant. We stopped halfway up the hill and beheld a Greek strawberry tree, its great brownish-red branches spraying out like a hydra's head. It was magnificent, and for a moment we just stared at this beautiful thing. Then Sahar directed our attention to the glyphs carved in its trunk: the calling card of a local Israeli militia. Sahar explained that these militiamen come as the feeling strikes them, vandalizing the land they believe to be their homeland, given to them by God. One night, Sahar and Nida were awakened by noises. They thought it might be a group of kids, but then the noises got louder, and when they went outside they saw that their house was surrounded by twenty or so settlers. The settlers ran when they saw Nida. But

they had already done their work—tools had been stolen, an oven destroyed, fish killed. Later, when I asked
Sahar how she and Nida live with this constant threat to
property and safety, she said:

> It is a precarious life. At the same time, there is a
> strong will to stay and keep working. There are
> communities whose villages are destroyed eighty
> times and they come back. It becomes part of
> how you live. It's a mode of survival. This is how
> you live on the land. We will keep going back,
> building the things they keep destroying.

We walked on, until we had completed our own
pilgrimage and reached the top of the hill. The sky was
wide open, with wisps of clouds floating by. A herd of
goats slowly made its way past us, and we watched as a
worker trained his attention on one particular goat lying
on the ground. It was in labor. The group of my fellow
writers circled the goat at a respectful distance and
watched in amazement as the worker midwifed two kids
slathered in the yellow goo of new life. Slightly amazed,
we walked inside one of the buildings, where I broke
away and wandered off on my own. I found myself in a
bedroom where I had been told artists are sometimes

welcome to spend a residency. I sat down on the fold-
out couch and for ten minutes conducted a residency of
my own. Outside I heard the goats bleating and my
comrades in conversation.

I thought back to our tour of Lydd, a city inside the
borders of Israel where in 1948 the nascent Israeli Defense Forces massacred a group of Palestinians by, among
other means, tossing grenades into a mosque. Our guide
there, Umar al-Ghubari, was concerned with the story
of the massacre and was also interested that it ran counter to Israel's own noble creation myth. The import of
this counternarrative, of Palestinian vindicationism, became clear once we reached the site of the massacre. We
stood on a traffic island across from the mosque, as our
guide narrated the events, citing the words of the Israeli
soldiers themselves. I looked over and saw an Israeli man
in dark glasses standing off to the side of our little group.
I knew he was Israeli only because of how he glared at
our guide as he recited the history of the site. At first, I
had the same semi-shocked reaction I have back home
when those in power so violently object to words. It
seemed absurd. Umar did not have any guns or knives.
And he was standing on land firmly under Israel's rule.
Nevertheless, Umar presented a threat—the threat of

the storyteller who can, through words, erode the claims of the powerful.

"Every single empire in its official discourse has said that it is not like all the others," writes Edward Said.

> That its circumstances are special, that it has a mission to enlighten, civilize, bring order and democracy, and that it uses force only as a last resort. And, sadder still, there always is a chorus of willing intellectuals to say calming words about benign or altruistic empires, as if one shouldn't trust the evidence of one's eyes watching the destruction and the misery and death brought by the latest *mission civilizatrice*.

Within days of publishing "The Case for Reparations," I began to feel the mistake. But it took years for the depth of that mistake, and thus my own debt, to compound. I felt it acutely atop that hill, and the mistake was far deeper than merely selecting the wrong model. My case for reparations was built on a chain of cases stretching back through James Forman, Queen Mother Moore, and Callie House, all the way back to Belinda Royall at the very founding of the United

States. In this sense, the case was not even mine; it was ancestral. And its target was one of the world's most malevolent inventions—racialized slavery and everything that flowed from it. Ancestors are important to me—they live on for me, not as ghosts but through words. Very often, before I sit down to write, I read back through those words—through slave narratives, letters from freedmen, memoirs, or poems. I read the words aloud like an incantation: "Dear Dangerfield you cannot imagine how much I want to see you. Come as soon as you can . . ." "I had a constant dread that Mrs. Moore, her mistress, would be in want of money and sell my dear wife . . ." "I would much rather you would get married to some good man, for every time I gits a letter from you it tears me all to pieces . . ." And I feel a portion of what they felt—a portion of their love, rage, hope, despair—and that portion is the power I try to convey in my own writing. I am not alone. I am in a tradition.

All that week I listened to Palestinians invoking that tradition, invoking James Baldwin, Amiri Baraka, or Angela Davis, explaining how these writers and activists revealed something of their own struggle to them. And then each night, the festival's guests gathered for a reading or talk with local Palestinian writers and intellectuals. One night I sat in the audience and was shocked to see a Palestinian writer named Bekriah Mawasi quote one of my books on a panel. In that moment, I felt the warmth of solidarity, of "conquered peoples," as one of my comrades put it, finding each other across the chasm of oceans and experience. But as warm as that felt, I also knew that in meeting across the chasm, one of us had reached further than the other. I am a writer and a bearer of a tradition, a writer and a steward. And what I felt sitting there on top of that hill, in residency with myself, was that if my writing had soared, my steward-ship had faltered.

The next morning I left the festival and made my way from Ramallah to Jerusalem. I had to wait an extra hour or so for a taxi with the right color license plate, yellow, and so be allowed to cross through a checkpoint in Is-rael's wall and onto the road to Jerusalem on the other side. I made small talk with my driver, then retreated back into my thoughts of the journey so far. It was my sixth day in Palestine, but I felt like I had been here for months. The days were filled with tours, the nights with talks—even the meals felt like seminars. Some of this is just being abroad somewhere far from home. But most of it was the specificity of this place—how much it seemed to embody the West and its contradictions, its claims of democracy, its foundations in exploitation. Of all the worlds I have ever explored, I don't think any shone so bright, so intense, so immediately as Palestine.

But when the light cleared I had new eyes, and I could see my own words in new ways—and the words from which they were derived—the stories, columns, speeches, and talks presented by "willing intellectuals." So much seemed obvious. I now noted a symmetry in the bromides—that those who claimed Israel as the only democracy in the Middle East were just as likely to claim that America was the oldest democracy in the world. And both claims relied on excluding whole swaths of the population living under the rule of the state. Riding in that taxi toward Jerusalem, the truth of this struck me as undeniable. I'd spent most of my time in the Occupied Territories, a world of minority rule. But even in the state proper, caste reigned. Palestinians living in Israel have shorter lives, are poorer, and live in more violent neighborhoods. Certain neighborhoods in Israel are allowed to discriminate legally against Palestinian citizens by setting "admission committees." The committees, operating in 41 percent of all Israeli localities, are free to bar anyone lacking "social suitability" or

"compatibility with the social and cultural fabric."
Openly racist appeals are the norm, as when Benjamin
Netanyahu warned in 2015 that "the right-wing government is in danger. Arab voters are heading to the
polling stations in droves." For all my talk of being fooled
by the language of "Jewish democracy," it had been right
there the whole time. The phrase means what it says—
a democracy for the Jewish people and the Jewish people alone.

If the language I'd heard all my professional life had
been wrong, had been deceptive even, then what was
the language to describe the project I now saw? It's true
that "Jim Crow" was the first thing that came to mind,
if only because "Jim Crow" is a phrase that connotes an
injustice, a sorting of human beings, the awarding and
stripping of the rights of a population. Certainly, that
was some part of what I saw in Hebron, in Jerusalem, in
Lydd.

But it was not just the literal meaning of "Jim Crow,"
it was the feeling of the thing too. I say the words "Jim
Crow" and a casket opens before me, and inside is a boy
beaten out of his own humanity. I say "Jim Crow" and I
see the flag of slavery waving above a state capitol. I say
"Jim Crow" and I see men on a balcony of the Lorraine
Motel pointing toward the shot. I say "Jim Crow" and

Detroit Red turns to me and asks, "Who taught you to hate?" I say "Jim Crow" and I hear "poll tax," "redlining," "grandfather clause," "whites only," and each of these phrases conjures additional images too. But "Jim Crow" was the language of analogy, of translation, not the thing itself. As much as anything, my mission in Palestine was to grow new roots, to describe this new world, not as a satellite of my old world but as a world in and of itself.

I stopped in Jerusalem just long enough to check into my hotel. I allowed myself a very nice room—one with soft sheets and a bathtub. I would pay for this self-indulgence. But not yet. I had five more days abroad, and whereas for the first five days I'd had comrades who were having their own set of revelations, now I was alone. Part of me would have done anything to go home. I was familiar with that part—it was the part that always grouses about the rigors of reporting, the awkwardness of asking strangers intimate questions, the discipline of listening intently. The voice is only in my head—but it was louder in Palestine. The days were longer and the revelations more intense. I remember walking up an inclining street in Hebron and reaching a large metal fence with a revolving gate. At the top of the gate was a device about the size of a shoebox with a tube protruding from it. It looked like a camera. In fact, it was a turret designed to lock on and immobilize a target using "nonlethal" rounds fired via remote control. The device's name—"Smart Shooter"—was written on the side. This was oppression's avant-garde—the first initial steps to automated imperial dominance—and I had little reason to feel that such trailblazing efforts would remain in Palestine. And at that I despaired.

I was away for ten days, ten days in this Holy Land of barbed wire, settlers, and outrageous guns. And every day I was there, I had a moment of profound despair. I truly wanted to look away, to go home and mumble some words about what I had seen in private. And maybe if I were left alone to my own devices, maybe if I were loyal only to myself, I would have done it. But I am a writer, and a bearer. I am a writer and a steward. I am not alone, and I don't just mean ancestors but the people I met every day living in abeyance of Israeli rule.

And I was not done. I took the elevator down to the lobby, where I met Avner Gvaryahu, who leads Breaking the Silence, a group of former IDF soldiers who now oppose the occupation. We walked outside, where an old pickup truck idled in front of the hotel. The driver, Guy Batavia, wore a baseball cap and thick glasses. We exchanged greetings, then I slid into the truck and we drove off.

My hosts were both Israeli—as nearly all my guides would be for the second half of my trip. This was a conscious decision. What it was not was an empty declaration to "hear both sides." I had no interest in defense of the occupation and what struck me then as segregation. Journalists claim to be hearing "both sides" as though a binary opposition had been set down by some disinterested god. But it is the journalists themselves who are playing god—it is the journalists who decide which sides are legitimate and which are not, which views shall be considered and which pushed out of the frame. And this power is an extension of the power of other curators of the culture—network execs, producers, publishers—whose core job is deciding which stories get told and which do not. When you are erased from the argument and purged from the narrative, you do not exist. Thus the complex of curators is doing more than setting pub dates and greenlighting—they are establishing and monitoring a criterion for humanity. Without this criterion, there can be no oppressive power, because the first duty of racism, sexism, homophobia, and so forth is the framing of who is human and who is not. But there is space beyond the brackets. For me it is a world of *Emerge* and "Evening Exchange," of barbershops and Baltimore Afros, a land where *The Last Dragon* is a classic teen movie and Lake Trout is heritage. What I have always wanted is to expand the frame of humanity, to shift the brackets of images and ideas. So that in thinking about my trip, in setting my sides upon the field, my frame excluded any defense of the patently immoral. And I would sooner hear a defense of cannibalism than I would hear any brief for what I saw with my own eyes in Hebron.

We drove from the hotel until we reached Highway 60, the "Way of the Patriarchs," an ancient road said to have been traveled by the Biblical prophets all the way south to Hebron. For much of this leg, Guy was silent as Avner described his time in the Israeli Defense Forces enforcing the occupation. I now hear this word—*occupation*—in the same way I might hear a middle-aged man speak of his "medical procedure" when what he means is "colonoscopy." The constant threat of violence, the stories I'd heard, by then did not seem fit for something as clinical as an "occupation." But Avner did not relish euphemism, and more than "occupation" he spoke of its tools—arrests, checkpoints, intelligence files, home invasion.

He said,

Every house in the Occupied Territories has a number. The number gives you basic intel on the people inside the house. If the people inside the house are somehow involved in any resistance, if someone in the family was imprisoned, if anyone was even blacklisted, that's a house *you will not take,* because then you're risking your troops. So you enter houses of people you know in advance are innocent. Now, we never called Palestinians "innocent." They were always "involved" or "not involved," because no one's "innocent."

You go into a house of that family and you basically use that house as your own as a military post. It's elevated, it's protected, but it's also sort of the eye in the sky for the soldiers on the ground. There's no privacy. There's obviously no warrant. You don't need to ask in advance. You don't call in advance. You don't send an email. You just barge in and usually handcuff and blindfold the head of the family. If there's a teenager who looks at you the wrong way or an uncle who looks big enough that he could threaten you, you do the same. . . . You disconnect the phones, close the curtains, so they won't tell anyone that you're there with them and they sit inside scared, petrified with their heads down.

This struck me as something out of a horror movie—a family held hostage not for ransom but as a show of the kind of dominance that is essential to Israeli rule. When the two-state solution seemed at hand, the thought was that Gaza, East Jerusalem, and the West Bank would be the territorial basis of a Palestinian state. The West Bank was subsequently divided into three zones—Area A, where Palestinians governed the civil authorities and enforced the law; Area B, which was to be governed jointly; and Area C, which would remain under Israeli control. This all sounds civilized enough, but that notion could not survive contact with a map. Area A holds most of the West Bank's population, but the entire zone is effectively an archipelago, filled with densely populated villages and urban centers, and more resembles an ink-blot test than the basis of a state. Area B is tiny and mostly rings the outskirts of towns. Area C, where Israeli power is complete, constitutes the only contiguous territory and the majority of the land, including the mineral-rich Jordan Valley. These distinctions are more of shading than of bright lines. The fact is that the West Bank is occupied, meaning Israel exercises its will wherever it chooses.

The tools of control are diverse—drones and observation towers surveil from above; earth mounds and trenches block the roads below. Gates enclose. Checkpoints inspect. Nothing is predictable. A road that was free yesterday is now suddenly impeded by a "flying checkpoint," a mobile gate and a squad of soldiers requesting permits and papers. But the randomness is intentional. The point is to make Palestinians feel the hand of occupation constantly—in Israel, in East Jerusalem, Area A, B, or C. "It's not just 'We're here and you're there,'" Avner told me, describing the relationship between the IDF and Palestinians in every jurisdiction. "It's 'We're here, and we're there.'"

In this way, a people is sundered from itself, and old communal bonds are eroded. The cousin who was once just down the road is walled off. What was once, in living memory, a long walk to court a potential wife in another village is transformed into an impossible obstacle course. And this is built upon the sundering that began in 1948—the sectioning off of Palestinians in Israel proper from those in East Jerusalem, and those in

East Jerusalem from those in the West Bank, and those in the West Bank from those in Gaza, and those in Gaza from the world.

He said:

> I remember this one mission I was in: go in, take control, the whole procedure. We're in the window doing what we're supposed to do, looking out the window. And then one of my soldiers, I was a sergeant, so one of my soldiers sort of calls up and says, "Hey, hey. Come quickly, I need your help."
>
> And I got there, and the situation was a father, standing with his daughter in his own home, trying to take her to the bathroom. And my soldier was standing there with his gun cocked in the face of the father, and his daughter is standing there between his legs, petrified. When I got there, she had already peed in her pants.
>
> That was sort of one of those moments where I was like, "What the fuck are we doing? Who is this for?"

Writing all of this now casts the illusion that I understood how the pieces of knowledge connected—

Avner's stories, the byzantine lines of occupation, the bromides, the articles. But they came together in moments. Sometimes I would be riding past a checkpoint and look out and, to my shock, see a young soldier with his rifle pointed at the road, which is to say at me. As soon as I would see this, I would search for a good reason, a justification, but eventually I started to realize there never was one. Even as I listened to Avner talk, even as we sped easily and unimpeded down roads that Palestinians on the West Bank cannot use, part of me was still searching. I did this because the weight of evil is so great. I did this because if the worst was true, if I was forced to see it square, then I knew what must come next. I did this because "a good reason" is also a way out. The weakness in me is always talking. But so are my ancestors.

We turned off Route 60 into the Israeli settlement of Kiryat Arba. A guard who seemed to be of East Asian descent held us at the checkpoint for a moment. Avner handed him his ID, and they talked in Hebrew; then the guard let us in. Guy parked the truck, and I followed Avner out into Kahane Park—a small garden named for Meir Kahane, the Jewish supremacist who as leader of the Kahanist movement (and a member of the Knesset) promoted the permanent annexation of the West Bank and Gaza and the enslavement of Palestinians. Kahane's political party was banned by the government in 1985, and he was assassinated in New York in 1990, but his disciple Baruch Goldstein took up his mantle. Four years after Kahane's death, Goldstein entered the Ibrahimi Mosque in Hebron and gunned down twenty-nine Muslims while they were worshipping. In the park, we stopped to look at a small cylindrical memorial to Kahane and then walked a few paces more until we reached a massive stone slab raised just above the ground. It was the tomb of Baruch Goldstein, and across its top were twenty or so small stones. Avner explained that this grave is a kind of shrine, regularly visited by those who see Goldstein as a martyr. Kahane and Goldstein were both officially pariahs—Kahane was shot in Manhattan, and Goldstein's mass murder was condemned by the Israeli government. But whatever one wishes to make of the official denunciations of Kahane and Goldstein, I was standing in a park bearing Kahane's name in which he and his mass-murdering acolyte were memorialized, a park that rested in a settlement sanctioned and subsidized by the state that claims to denounce him.

Goldstein's rampage was stopped by the Palestinian

worshippers themselves, who rose up, disarmed him, and beat him to death. In the wake of the street protests that exploded in the city, Israel segregated the streets of Hebron and set curfews for its Palestinian residents. To this very day, the legacy of that crackdown endures. Walking the streets of Hebron, as I had, seeing the shuttered storefronts and the soldiers patrolling the streets, it was hard to avoid the feeling that Goldstein had won. And this feeling held true for me across the West Bank, where the pace of colonization and settlement had expanded, not declined, since the 1994 massacre. In 1993, when the Oslo Peace Accords were signed, the settler population was 111,000. Today it's half a million.

Goldstein and the subsequent Israeli reaction to Palestinian unrest in Hebron are manifestations of an uncomfortable reality: This putative "Jewish democracy" is, like its American patron, an expansionist power. Zionism demands, as Levi Eshkol, prime minister of Israel during the 1960s, once put it, "the dowry, not the bride"—that is to say, the land without the Palestinians on it. And every expansionist power needs a good story to justify its plunder.

Whatever connections formed in my mind between the Israeli oppression and American segregation, Israel's version did not make the case for itself in the language of Jim Crow but in the dialect of liberal expansionism—with its descriptions of barbaric natives and promises of the great improvements brought to the savages by their betters. The father of Zionism, Theodor Herzl, first considered Argentina, believing that it would be in that "sparsely populated" country's "highest interest . . . to cede us a portion of its territory." When Herzl turned to Palestine, he viewed Palestinians, as historian Benny Morris puts it, as little more than "part of the scenery." The scenery was savage: "We should form a portion of a rampart of Europe against Asia," Herzl wrote in his 1896 manifesto, *The Jewish State*. "An outpost of civilization against barbarism."

A year earlier, Herzl claimed in a diary entry that Zionism would ultimately benefit those whose lands he sought to occupy; further, "it goes without saying" that those who sought to raise the banner of civilization would still "respectfully tolerate persons of other faiths and protect their property, their honor and their freedom." Such protections would set for "the entire world a wonderful example." But this benevolent spirit was undercut by the marching orders Herzl offered in that same entry:

We must expropriate gently the private property on the estates assigned to us. We shall try to spirit the penniless population across the border by procuring employment for it in the transit countries, while denying it any employment in our own country. **The property owners will come over to our side.** Both the process of expropriation and the removal of the poor must be carried out discreetly and circumspectly.

Herzl's writing fits well within Said's "official discourse" of empire, where expropriation and banishment are presented as a species of altruism and tolerance. Herzl died in 1904, but by then what he called "a gigantic dream" had assumed a force of its own. And some of his most influential followers thought it better to dispense with the vocabulary of liberal conquest and speak plainly. In his 1923 essay "The Iron Wall," Zionist theorist Ze'ev Jabotinsky wrote that the "Jewish colonist" who imagined that "the Arab race" would "voluntarily consent to the realization of Zionism" was exhibiting condescending contempt. Better to name the thing flat out:

My readers have a general idea of the history of colonization in other countries. I suggest that they consider all the precedents with which they are acquainted and see whether there is one solitary instance of any colonization being carried on with the consent of the native population.

It's worth lingering on Jabotinsky's invocation of "colonization." Modern Zionists recoil in horror at any association between their own ideology and colonialism. They claim "the Land of Israel" as their homeland, and from there assert that no people can colonize their own home.

This formulation evinces, at best, a deep ignorance of the history of Israel's patron state. In 1816, a group of white elites decided that, in the matter of Black people, ethnic cleansing would be preferred to enslavement. The American Colonization Society was formed with the explicit goal of shipping as many Blacks as possible back to their national home—Africa. The ACS garnered some support in Black communities, terrorized by racist whites much as the Jews of Europe were terrorized by antisemitic Europeans. And much as Jewish Zionists saw themselves bringing the boon of "civilization" to Palestine, Black American colonizers of Africa believed they would do the same. Thus Liberia was born—and plagued, for much of its history, by its colonial past.

As for an "anticolonial" Zionism, if such a thing could be spoken of it would come as a shock to the ideology's founders. "The land of our fathers is waiting for us; let us colonize it," wrote Eliezer Ben-Yehuda, linguist and godfather of modern Hebrew, in 1880. "And, by becoming its masters, we shall again be a people like all others." This mastering of the land meant economic control. Zionist Ber Borochov urged Jews to assume "the leading position in the economy of the new land" in 1906, and in this way "Jewish immigration may be diverted to colonization of the undeveloped country." And mastery also meant violence. While many Zionists spoke of peaceful accord between their aims and the aims of Palestinians, Jabotinsky never allowed himself the liberty of such euphemism:

> There is no such precedent. . . . The native populations, civilised or uncivilised, have always stubbornly resisted the colonists, irrespective of whether they were civilised or savage.

But "the native population" *was* savage, and Jabotinsky saw a clear difference between the Jewish colonizer and the Arabs to be colonized. "Culturally they are five hundred years behind us," wrote Jabotinsky. "They have neither our endurance nor our determination." The early Zionists might have considered the land of Palestine as their rightful homeland, but they never imagined themselves as "natives." Natives, in colonial discourse, were savages with no capacity to improve the land and thus no right to it. In 1943, as Zionist terrorist groups led an insurgency against British rule, their commander and the future prime minister of Israel, Menachem Begin, learned that one of their soldiers had been flogged by the British. "Jews are not Zulus," wrote Begin. "You will not whip Jews in their homeland."

Begin's delineation—separating Jewish redeemers from the uncivilized natives—was reinforced by the West. In 1946, a British and American alliance dispatched an "Anglo-American Committee of Inquiry" to decide upon the fate of Mandatory Palestine, as well as its six hundred thousand Jews and 1.1 million non-Jews. In Jaffa, the delegates wrote of an "overgrown Arab village" filled with "squalor and a population diseased and beaten by life." But in Jewish Tel Aviv they marveled at the "thoroughly civilized community" with its "tree-shaded boulevards, with opera and theaters, with playgrounds and modern schools, with busses and apartment houses." Zionism would free the Arab race from "the veil, the fez, the sickness, the filth, the lack of education."

This narrative of a barbaric Palestine plagued by filth and chaos, as contrasted with an ostensibly pristine and orderly West, has never faded. In 2013, Israeli journalist Ari Shavit published *My Promised Land*, a bestselling apologia for Zionism in which he tracks his great-grandfather's 1897 voyage into Mandatory Palestine. In Shavit's telling, his ancestor arrives into "the chaos of Arab Jaffa." This is a city of squalor—of "hanging animal carcasses, the smelly fish, the rotting vegetables" and "the infected eyes of the village women," one where Shavit's ancestor is forced to contend with "the hustling, the noise, the filth." Jaffa is not unique. In Jerusalem, this ancestor is faced with "the misery of the Orient: dark, crooked alleyways, filthy markets, hungry masses."

This is an amazing account, if only because Shavit's ancestor was coming from London—a city so notoriously filthy that it was nicknamed "The Great Smoke."

In his book *Dirty Old London*, Lee Jackson sketches the city:

Thoroughfares were swamped with black mud, composed principally of horse dung, forming a tenacious, glutinous paste; the air was peppered with soot, flakes of filth tumbling to the ground "in black Plutonian show'rs." The distinctive smell of the city was equally unappealing. Winter fogs brought mephitic sulphurous stinks. The summer months, on the other hand, created their own obnoxious cocktail, "that combined odour of stale fruit and vegetables, rotten eggs, foul tobacco, spilt beer, rank cart-grease, dried soot, smoke, triturated road-dust and damp straw." London was the heart of the greatest empire ever known; a financial and mercantile hub for the world; but it was also infamously filthy.

Jackson understands London's sanitation problems structurally—from 1801 to 1901, the city's population grew from one million to six million. But Shavit's narrative of Jaffa's sanitation problems is about the people *themselves.*

The Anglo-American Committee delegates understood Zionism to be the "inevitable giving way of a backward people before a more modern and practical one." But more, they saw in it a formative episode in their own history—the "conquest of Indians." Zionists and their allies agreed. Jabotinsky believed the Arab race possessed "the same instinctive jealous love of Palestine, as the old Aztecs felt for ancient Mexico, and the Sioux for their rolling Prairies." Inveighing against British rule of Mandatory Palestine, Progressive Henry Wallace wrote that the British were "stirring up the Arabs," just as they had "stirred up the Iroquois to fight the [American] colonists."

The notion that a colonialist Zionism exists merely in the hallucinations of leftist professors and the chants of their wayward students ignores a crucial source—the very words of Zionists themselves. But Herzl, Jabotinsky, and Ben-Yehuda were of a time when it was still possible for the West to propagate an untrammeled image of a noble colonialism. That is no longer the case. We say "colonialism" and an American colonel replies, "I have come to kill Indians. . . . Kill and scalp all, big and little; nits make lice." We say "colonialism" and Cecil Rhodes strides across an entire continent. We say "colonialism" and a French interrogator attaches electrodes to the private parts of an Algerian man. We say "colonialism" and the settlers of Kiryat Arba materialize before us, giving thanks and praises for mass murder.

And there was so little shame in any of this. Some years ago, I went on a tour of Civil War sites in Tennessee. I visited Fort Pillow, where Nathan Bedford Forrest, founder of the Ku Klux Klan, massacred a unit of Black soldiers. I watched Confederate reenactors in all their regalia. I listened to the lectures of the Sons of Confederate Veterans. It was all propaganda, and I knew it. But I had not yet learned the lesson I brought with me to Palestine. I did not yet understand my own faculties, that I had the right to set my brackets as I would in Palestine and shove bullshit—no matter how politely articulated, no matter how elegantly crafted—out of the frame. And then one evening, after a long day, I showed up to dinner and saw a group brandishing the Confederate battle flag. I don't know what got ahold of me. I don't know why it was right then. But I understood that this was a matter not of public history but of deep belief. I quietly excused myself and went to my room. Even then I remember not wanting to make a scene or in anyway disturb my hosts. But the next morning, they apologized profusely. They knew.

When I think back to that trip, what I see now is varying degrees of shame—conscious and unconscious. At Fort Pillow there was an interpretive film that, all at once, sought to celebrate Forrest and the Black soldiers he massacred. The Sons of Confederate Veterans kept

talking about an old graveyard for the enslaved that they were restoring. The reenactors spoke vaguely about the cause for which they fought. And after that display of the Confederate flag, what my hosts seemed to fear the most had less to do with the flag of slavery and more to do with some sense that they, as white Southerners, had appeared in the exact manner that "Yankees" expected—as ignorant, uncouth, or ill-bred.

They didn't have to worry. I've known too many "Yankee" racists and well-bred fools. And it was good for me to see them as they would be without me—the comfort they showed with a flag that only a few years later would be claimed by Dylann Roof. Sometimes, you are blessed with a moment where all the dissembling, all the shame, all the politesse are stripped, and evil speaks with clarity. Sometimes it's in a park named for a nineteenth-century slave trader. And sometimes it's in a settlement that honors a twentieth-century advocate of that same system. In either case, the clarity is a gift and we should listen close. In this memorial to Meir Kahane and his disciple, the gift spoke of Israel's deeper designs.

Settlements like Kiryat Arba are not the work of rogue pioneers; much like our own redlined suburbs, they are state projects. In the settlements, first-time homebuyers are eligible for subsidized mortgages at low interest rates to build houses on land they lease at discounted rates—a discount made possible on account of the land being stolen. Factories and farms are propped by a similar array of discounts and subsidies. All infrastructure—roads, water, power, public synagogues, and mikvahs—is paid for by the state. In this web of subsidies is an incentive to further colonize the land of Palestinians, because further colonization advances a primary interest of the Israeli state—the erosion of any grounds for a future Palestinian state.

Standing there looking at Goldstein's grave, having visited Al-Haram Al-Ibrahimi only a few days earlier, I felt the horror of Goldstein's spectacular violence intimately. But what I was beginning to see was that settlement, itself, was violent. When Israel constructs settlements in the West Bank, it extends its borders past the settlements—sometimes onto Palestinian farmland. Palestinian access to this land is almost always contested, and generally granted based on a maze of permits or the mood of the security forces who guard the settlements. In any clash between Palestinians and settlers, the soldiers can be expected to take the side of the settlers. And the settlers are, themselves, often armed perpetrators of violence. "The settlements play a political and a strategic role in taking over land," Avner explained. "Imagine a pond. You throw a rock in a pond and it creates a ripple, right? The settlements create a ripple effect of violence everywhere they are. That's the way they're built."

What I could now see was something more than bad actors or individual zealots but a system at work. I asked Avner and Guy how they could reconcile living under that system with the Zionism responsible for their very existence. There was quiet in the car for a moment. Avner answered first. He said he believed in self-determination for the Jewish people and that questions of where that self-determination should play out were now theoretical. "We're here," he said. "The question is, can there be a way to have the right to self-determination for Israelis and to Palestinians? I think the answer is yes, there has to be. I mean, there's no other way. But I do think that there are very dangerous things that have grown out of this concept of Jewish nationality, which has transformed into Jewish superiority or Jewish supremacy, which goes beyond Kahane or Goldstein. I mean, this is deeply rooted within Israeli society, within Zionist ideology. There is a wish and a want for self-determination. I don't think that's inherently wrong. I think what's inherently wrong is one nationality coming at the expense of the other. That's sort of my attempt . . ."

Avner trailed off. Guy did not speak of such pragmatics. "For myself, I understand that I see the establishment of Israel as a sin. I don't think it should have happened," he said. He spoke of Israel as "a center of Jewish supremacy," which he did not see changing. "So, it's something that I can't live with. And I think that in order to have some kind of sustainable, reasonable life here, there should be a real change."

When I was young, I felt the physical weight of race constantly. We had less. Our lives were more violent. And whether by genes, culture, or divine judgment, this was said to be our fault. The only tool to escape this damnation—for a lucky few—was school. Later I went out into the world and saw the other side, those who allegedly, by genes, culture, or divine judgment, had more but—as I came to understand—knew less. These people, white people, were living under a lie. More, they were, in some profound way, suffering for the lie. They had seen more of the world than I had—but not more of humanity itself. Most stunningly, I realized that they were deeply ignorant of their own country's history, and thus they had no intimate sense of how far their country could fall. A system of supremacy justifies itself through illusion, so that those moments when the illusion can no longer hold always come as a great shock. The Trump years amazed a certain kind of white person; they had no reference for national vulgarity, for such broad corruption and venality, until it was too late. The least reflective of them say, "This is not America." But some of them suspect that it *is* America, and there is great pain in understanding that, without your consent, you are complicit in a great crime, in learning that the whole game was rigged in your favor, that there are nations within your nation who have spent all of their collective lives in the Trump years. The pain is in the discovery of your own illegitimacy—that whiteness is power and nothing else. I could hear that same pain in Avner's and Guy's words. They were raised under the story that the Jewish people were the ultimate victims of history. But they had been confronted with an incredible truth—that there was no ultimate victim, that victims and victimizers were ever flowing.

It was late morning. We were now approaching the town of Susya, in the South Hebron Hills, toward the edge of the West Bank. This "town" was a makeshift collection of perhaps twenty shacks and outbuildings across a strip of land. Susya native and activist Nasser Nawaj'ah welcomed us into the living room of his modest home. We sat down on the couch, and he served us tea.

Susya is in that broad swath of land deemed to be Area C, where Israelis have total control. The vast majority of settlements are in Area C, and it was here that the ripples of violence Avner spoke of were the most intense. But open, direct violence is just one of the tools of land theft on the West Bank. What I was beginning to see was an arsenal of weaponry—highway construction, water restriction, gated villages, forbidden streets, checkpoints, soldiers, settlers—all employed to part the dowry from the bride. I would catch myself marveling at the elegance of it all, the way one marvels at an ingenious bank robbery. But then I would meet people like Nasser—people whose life savings were the land—and I would be reminded of the sin of abstraction, which was, after all, the very sin I'd perpetrated in my work.

I was told that the people of Susya and the broader region of Masafer Yatta have historically dwelled in caves. But "cave," with its Neanderthal implications, does not quite describe what I saw in Masafer Yatta. Imagine homes made of stone and earth, improved with electricity and plumbing and sectioned into rooms.

These "cave" homes have the great utility of being durable against the volatile weather that marks the region. Nasser's ancestors had lived in such homes since the eighteenth century. Nasser himself had been born into one, but the scheme of dowry divided from bride had placed him in the small slight housing where we were now received.

In 1982, when Nasser was just a baby, a group of Israeli visitors came to visit the original village. The villagers greeted the people warmly—there was tea, just as I was being served now. But later it became clear that the "visitors" were running reconnaissance. Having discovered an ancient synagogue on the land, Israel declared the village of Susya an archaeological site. The state placed the management of the site in the hands of local settlers, who immediately moved to push the Palestinian residents out of their homes and off the land. Nasser's people were dispersed across the West Bank. Nasser's family moved to their farmland to the south, hoping to find solace there. But they were now hemmed in between the settler-controlled archaeological site and an actual settlement. And then there was the law.

Land in Israel and the areas where it has direct control—Jerusalem and most of the West Bank—are tightly managed by the state. In much of the country, land cannot be outright purchased but must be leased from the state. And in Area C, communities must submit an application, with an attendant array of documents, aerial photos, and legal briefs, to receive a lease. The adjudicators of the process, like the managers of the Susya archaeological site and the judges who handle appeals, are often themselves settlers who are living in the colonies of the West Bank. Nonetheless, Nasser's people submitted a plan, including an application, to have their new community recognized by the planning commission in Area C. This went nowhere, and at that point Nasser's people abandoned working through the system. "Why submit? The whole committees are against us," he told me. "These are settler-led communities. There's no Palestinian representatives."

The camp where Nasser now lives is illegal, meaning that, at any moment, Israeli bulldozers could appear and demolish everything. But the bureaucracy that rules over Susya still has its own opaque internal rules. For now, instead of taking down the entire camp, they have settled for demolishing one structure at a time. The result is a kind of limbo—Nasser goes to bed every night not knowing whether his roof will be collapsed in upon him and his family. A few years ago, a massive blizzard hit the South Hebron Hills, destroying many of the village's shelters. Families spent the night shoveling snow out of their housing. "One of our residents has a heart condition, and this was during this blizzard, and we called the police to help," he said. "It's so rare that we as Palestinians would call the forces of the occupation to help us. But we called them because he had a heart condition. They didn't come."

Fortunately, the man lived. But after the blizzard passed and Nasser's people went back to rebuilding their camp, settlers took pictures of the rebuilding and submitted them for approval to a judge—who was himself a settler. But what bothered Nasser the most was that his people had originally moved into the caves precisely because of their durability against harsh weather. "There's no justice for Palestinians," Nasser said in reference to the courts. "It's the opposite. Lack of justice. The courts are a tool of the oppressor, a tool of the occupation."

Susya is only still standing because Nasser and his community have been able to attract international attention. The need to keep up appearances, to pose as a modern Western state, leaves Israel somewhat vulnerable to international pressure. But the international context that most occupied Nasser at that moment was a very particular one. "I see this as apartheid," he said.

The evening after my trip to Susya, I caught a ride up to Tel Aviv with a friend. The tension of Jerusalem gave way to teeming cafés, wide boulevards, and glass towers. There was an air of the future that I would associate with a certain kind of liberal city back home, flush with mass transit and interesting restaurants and cocktail bars. The men were carefree in their tees and shades. The women were happy in their cut-off shorts. I took a seat at an outdoor café just off of Habima Square, watching as crowds of protesters, frustrated by Netanyahu's attempt to subjugate the country's courts, walked past waving Israeli flags. One of the flags subbed in pink and white for the traditional Israeli silhouette.

I ordered a ginger ale and then promptly began stewing. I was watching the ranks of protesters file past. But I was also thinking of all I'd seen the past few days—of Hebron, Susya, and the Old City—and how distant it felt from these protests. Back in America these protests enjoyed positive coverage and were taken as evidence of the vitality and mettle of "the only democracy in the Middle East." But by then I knew that "the only democracy in the Middle East" was essentially a tagline which, like "the Breakfast of Champions" or "Just do it," depended less on logic or observed reality than a form of word association. The "Middle East" is the insanity of suicide bombings, the backwardness of a woman peeking out from her niqab. "Democracy" is a flag over Iwo Jima, Washington crossing the Delaware, a working man rising in a town meeting. Overlay the two phrases and a collage emerges—a visual representation of Herzl's dream of "an outpost of civilization against barbarism." And this collage is a technology, as functional as any other: Who can judge democratic Israel, which must exist in "that part of the world" where child brides, chemical weapons, and bin Laden reign?

I sat there in the café raging in my own head, raging at this protest whose aim was the preservation of a democracy for some. But then I walked out into the crowd. There were flags, drums, chants, and a sense of fellowship among the protesters. The earnestness of it all made it hard to stay angry. These people were sincere. I thought back to my conversation with Avner and Guy and how hard it is to truly acknowledge your place in a system whose actions indict your conscience. But now, seeing the shape of my travels these past couple of years, I think of Josiah Nott, of D. W. Griffith, of all the literature assembled to hide the truth of an oppressive class from itself, to assure itself that it is indeed right with the universe.

The Zionist corpus is filled with such entries, and many of them are little more than analogues for America. The boats bringing fleeing Jews to Mandatory Palestine are referred to as "the Mayflowers of a whole generation," the combatants fighting to seize power from the British are likened to "the men of Concord or Lexington," and the phrase "It's 1776 in Palestine" is marshaled as a rallying cry. When the American journalist Frank W. Buxton visited a kibbutz as part of the 1946 Anglo-American Committee, what he saw was his own national genealogy. "I've always been proud of my own ancestors who made farms out of the virgin forest," Buxton said. "But these people are raising crops out of rocks!" The sense, that if Buxton's ancestors had created a state out of an unpopulated void so could the Zionists, predated Buxton. In 1881, as a wave of pogroms was unleashed on Russian Jews, American clergyman William E. Blackstone despaired that "these millions cannot remain where they are, and yet have no other place to go." But for Blackstone the tragedy was compounded by the fact that there was an obvious solution to the Land of Palestine—"a land without a people, and a people without a land."

Blackstone gave language, pithy and poetic, to an idea that would recur repeatedly in Zionist thought: that the Palestinian people did not exist. "It was not as though there was a Palestinian people in Palestine, considering itself as a Palestinian people and we came and threw them out and took their country from them," argued Golda Meir. Buried in the claim is another notion—that the worth of a people is defined by their possession of a homeland incorporated as a state. The Palestinians, lacking such a state, had no right to the land and perhaps no rights at all. The charge of being without a homeland or "stateless" was often lodged at Jews themselves. Zionists sought to answer that charge, but they did not dispute its premise. Their model was America's pilgrims or Minutemen, and the role they saw for Palestinians was thus predictable.

In 1958 Leon Uris published his bestselling novel *Exodus,* which was later adapted into a movie starring Paul Newman. Uris hated any depiction of "weak Jews" and believed that many Israelis felt the same due to their "strong feelings about Jews who will not fight back." And the people that they were to fight back against was clear. "This is Israel," wrote Uris in a 1956 letter to his father, the "fighter who spits in the eye of the Arab hordes and dares him." Thus, the Jewish people could restore the honor lost to the Nazis by warring against Arabs in the breach. But better than substitute Nazis, the Palestinians gave Israel *savage* Nazis, third-world barbarians embodying the depraved native in the colonial mind. The Aztec. The Indian. The Zulu. The Arab. In *Exodus,* the image of marauding Arabs, cowardly and prone to rape, will be familiar to anyone who has seen the depiction of Black people in Griffith's *Birth of a Nation.* For just as the vulgar caricature of Black people served the cause of white Redemption, so too did the Arabs in *Exodus* serve the cause of Zionism.

A fan of the Western genre, Uris wrote *Exodus* to appeal to American "gentiles." The reception for his book, which dovetailed with the cause of Israeli redemption, was rapt. Nine years after *Exodus*'s publication, the Six-Day War consecrated an American martial love of Israel. It was 1967, and America was embroiled in a war with a colonized enemy in which it was losing both the physical battles and the moral high ground. But in Israel, Americans saw Western warriors vanquishing the savages. These were not soldiers but righteous, reluctant defenders of a long-persecuted people, killing only when forced to the brink.

In Israel, this ideal was summed up in the IDF's concept of "Purity of Arms." Drawn from its official code of ethics, "Purity of Arms" holds that Israeli soldiers are particularly noble when fighting with restraint and maintaining their "humanity even in combat." In America, journalists ran with this notion and fashioned their own Lost Cause of the IDF. In the September 1967 issue of *The Atlantic,* in an article titled "The Swift Sword," Barbara Tuchman wrote of Israeli soldiers "fighting and crying," describing them as "lions" who "fought with tears" while assuring her readers that the Israelis, because of their own history, were a different kind of army. "The Jewish people are not accustomed to conquest, and we receive it with mixed feelings," General Yitzhak Rabin told Tuchman.

When *A Distant Mirror* was published years later, Tuchman warned against a hagiography of violence, citing the knights of that period:

> King Arthur's knights adventured for the right against dragons, enchanters, and wicked men, establishing order in a wild world. So their living counterparts were supposed, in theory, to serve as defenders of the Faith, upholders of justice, champions of the oppressed. In practice, they were themselves the oppressors, and by the 14th cen-

tury the violence and lawlessness of men of the sword had become a major agency of disorder.

But back in 1967, the story of this seemingly ragtag force fighting honorably and crying while shooting proved too seductive. As did the urge to apply the most disreputable pseudoscience of that era.

The Anglo-American Committee saw in Israelis a transformation—"a new generation of Jews rising free from the stigma of the ghetto"—that was not just spiritual but physical. "Many of the Jewish children I saw were blond and blue-eyed, a mass mutation that, I was told, is yet to be adequately explained," wrote the committee's commissioner, Bartley Crum. "It is the more remarkable because the majority of the Jews of Palestine are of east European Jewish stock, traditionally dark-haired and dark-eyed. One might almost assert that a new Jewish folk is being created in Palestine." In 1951, journalist Kenneth W. Bilby wrote that the Israeli Jews were becoming physically separate from "their Semitic cousin in the Arab world." After visiting with a group of children in a kibbutz, Bilby wrote, "I would have defied any anthropologist to mix these children with a crowd of British, American, German and Scandinavian youngsters and then weed out the Jews."

Bilby's note speaks to the racecraft at work in the West, and to the absurd boundaries of whiteness and Jews' uncertain place within it. The war that resulted in so much Jewish death, World War II, was as much a race war as a world war—one with deep roots in America. As early as 1905, the German conquerors of South West Africa instituted antimiscegenation laws—laws they'd adopted from their studies of the American South. Later, when the Germans sought to inaugurate their extermination of the Herero and the Nama, their reasoning was clear: "The natives must give way," the German general Lothar von Trotha remarked. "Look at America." In the 1930s, when the Nazis sought precedent for their battery of antisemitic laws, they found it in America—the world's "leading racist jurisdiction," writes historian James Q. Whitman. The relatively small presence of Black people proved no barrier for Nazis. Hitler "saw the entire world as an 'Africa,'" writes historian Timothy Snyder. "And everyone, including Europeans, in racial terms." Ukrainians and Poles were derided as "blacks." Slavs were said to fight "like Indians." And the Germans imagined themselves as heroic colonizers, "tamers of distant lands," writes Snyder. Among those nations under Hitler's boot, the message was not missed.

"We are like slaves," a Ukrainian woman wrote in her diary. "Often the book *Uncle Tom's Cabin* comes to mind. Once we shed tears over those Negroes, now obviously we ourselves are experiencing the same thing."

In the immediate postwar years, the place of Jews in the tent of whiteness was still uncertain. Even after the Holocaust, antisemitism remained a powerful force, and in the camps where those dislocated by the war huddled, Jewish "Displaced Persons" found themselves in filthy, prisonlike conditions complete with barbed wire. "As matters stand," wrote American official Earl G. Harrison in a report on the camps, "we appear to be treating the Jews as the Nazis treated them except that we do not exterminate them." This treatment was not incidental but reflective of a deep-seated hatred that reached the highest levels of authority in the camps. Apprised of Harrison's report, General George S. Patton, who commanded the Displaced Persons camps in Bavaria, fumed in his diary that "Harrison and his ilk believe that the Displaced Person is a human being, which he is not, and this applies particularly to the Jews who are lower than animals."

If the average American was less rabid in their antisemitism, that spelled no great sympathy for the

Holocaust's survivors. In a 1945 poll, only 5 percent of Americans believed that immigration should be increased, while 37 percent believed immigration should be further restricted. When Congress, at President Truman's behest, attempted to adjust its immigration laws to allow for more Displaced Persons to enter the country, Texas Congressman Ed Gossett denounced them as "the refuse of Europe." His office was then flooded with a wave of antisemitic vitriol denouncing the "Jew dominated legislation," inveighing against the "Jew Deal," asserting that America had "fought on the wrong side" and that Jews had "ruined every country they ever entered including Germany," and were "already ruining the USA." Against this backdrop, Congress passed an immigration bill in 1948 that employed geographical and time restrictions in the hopes of keeping Jewish immigration to a minimum. That same year, the United States became the first country to recognize Israeli independence. The cause of Jewish whiteness was thus advanced by keeping "them over there"—and better still, over there warring against natives and savages.

Righteous violence vented on some brutish, blighted lower caste has always been the key to entry into the fraternity of Western nations. And when those nations feel themselves humiliated, when their national honor is stained, then that venting is at its most terrible. No people in this world were made to understand this more than Hitler's ultimate *Untermenschen*—the Jews of Europe. Uris's rage at "weak Jews," those who during the Holocaust refused to "fight back," echoed a sentiment found in some quarters of the Jewish community. Mordechai Gichon fought in World War II in the U.K.'s Jewish Brigade and subsequently encountered survivors of Nazi atrocities. He was left with as much shame as sympathy:

> My brain could not grasp, not then and not today, how it could have been that there were tens of thousands of Jews in a camp with only a few German guards. But they did not rise up, they simply went like lambs to the slaughter. . . . Why didn't they tear [the Germans] to shreds? I've always said that no such thing could happen in the Land of Israel.

The wars against the Palestinians and their Arab allies were a kind of theater in which "weak Jews" who went "like lambs to slaughter" were supplanted by Israelis who would "fight back." Thus a redemption of a different kind was affected: By routing the savage "Arab," by murdering his leaders, by confining him to the Bantustans of Tuba, or the reservations of Gaza, or the ghettoes of Lydd, Jewish national honor was restored in the traditional manner of Western European powers. The "mass mutation" into whiteness was advanced, and "IDF," "Mossad," and "Shin Bet" all became synonyms for righteous manly violence. That definition is the product of done things—but the done thing had to be rendered. It needed Leon Uris's hatred of "weak Jews." It needed Barbara Tuchman's crying lions. And it needed both an American audience and American narrators. For the movie adaptation of *Exodus,* all-American pop star Pat Boone was selected to pen the lyrics for the theme song and perform them. Boone did not disappoint:

If I must fight, I'll fight to make this land our own
Until I die, this land is mine

Having vanquished its Arab foes and established itself as a state, Israel began the process of securing as much land as possible for its new state while keeping as many Palestinians as possible beyond that state's borders. This ethnocratic approach to state-building had deep roots in Zionism, which held that majority status within a strong Jewish state was the only true bulwark against antisemitism. Implanting this majority presented an obvious problem—the Palestinians. "There is only one thing the Zionists want, and it is that one thing that the Arabs do not want," wrote Jabotinsky,

> for that is the way by which the Jews would gradually become the majority, and then a Jewish Government would follow automatically, and the future of the Arab minority would depend on the goodwill of the Jews; and a minority status is not a good thing, as the Jews themselves are never tired of pointing out. So there is no "misunderstanding." The Zionists want only one thing, Jewish immigration; and this Jewish immigration is what the Arabs do not want.

By 1948, Israel no longer had to consider what "the Arabs" might want. Over seven hundred thousand Palestinians were uprooted from their own lands and banished by the advancing Israeli Army. Many of these people believed that they would be able to return to their homes after the war. But such a return would destroy the Israeli state project by turning Jews into a minority—the very thing Zionists sought to prevent. So the Palestinians were denied the "right of return," and their land was confiscated by the state and handed over to other Israelis. The transformation was stunning: Before the establishment of the Israeli state, Palestinians owned 90 percent of all land in Mandatory Palestine. Most of this land was seized and incorporated into Israel. "From 1948 to 1953, the five years following the establishment of the state, 350 (out of a total of 370) new Jewish settlements were built on land owned by Palestinians," writes Noura Erakat in her book *Justice for Some.*

The threat of losing demographic supremacy still hangs over Israel. In 2003, future prime minister Ehud Olmert called on Israel to "maximize the number of Jews" and "minimize the number of Palestinians." A "Muslim majority" would mean the "destruction of Israel as a Jewish state," claimed former prime minister Ehud Barak. Netanyahu once warned that if Palestinian citizens ever reached 35 percent of Israel, the Jewish state would be "annulled." Looking at the "absurd" borders of Jerusalem, the former deputy mayor Meron Benvenisti summarized the policy behind them as "the aspiration to include a maximum of land with a minimum of Arabs."

There is a direct relationship between this vulnerability, this fragility implicit in the Zionist Dream, and the great tension I felt on my first day in Jerusalem. The Old City is part of a larger group of surrounding communities called the Old City Basin. This region is home to some one hundred thousand Palestinians, as opposed to six thousand Israelis. There is not a larger concentration of sites holy to the Abrahamic religions on the planet than this region—and within it, the ratio of Palestinians to Israelis is twenty to one. Back in Susya, Nasser told me that when his family was kicked out of their home, the cave was converted into "a cinema" and "a tourist center" dedicated to "biblical time." As ever, the rush of information overwhelmed me and I had some difficulty imagining a cave that had once been someone's home being turned into a cinema and tourist center dedicated to biblical times. My mind conjured images of a planetarium with angels floating among the heavens and then an IMAX theater where Israeli hosts handed out black glasses so that one might see the prophets striding across the land in 3D. I dismissed these images as absurd.

But two days after I saw Nasser, Avner and I visited what I can only call an archaeological amusement park, the City of David—a sprawling complex on a hillside abutting the Old City of Jerusalem. We walked into a large, welcoming lobby filled with school-age Israeli kids laughing, yelling, and running. I purchased a ticket and then wandered into the heart of the complex, which was built around a portion of an archaeological dig dating back to the late nineteenth century, when the British first discovered evidence of an ancient settlement here that was older than the Old City itself. The British believed that the archaeology of the Holy Land would prove the historicity of the Bible and thus armor Christian faith with the gauntlets and greaves of empiricism and science. Shortly after uncovering evidence of this encampment, the British made a shocking declaration: They had discovered the seat of King David, slayer of Goliath, founder of the Judean dynasty, and progenitor of the ancient kingdom of Israel.

The Israeli writer and chronicler Amos Elon once described archaeology in Israel as "almost a national sport," which had captivated a nation forever looking for "the reassurance of roots." Elon noted that Israeli national symbols were almost wholly drawn from antiquities. "For the disquieted Israeli," Elon wrote, "the moral comforts of archaeology are considerable." Like that of the British before them, Zionist archaeology sought to affirm the Bible as history to affirm its state project. What that project needed was an unbroken narrative, stretching back to time immemorial, of Jewish nationhood. With such a narrative in hand, Israel would then have what Ben-Gurion called "the sacrosanct title-deed to Palestine."

As I made my way through the City of David, the evidence of this title deed, much less the presence of the ancient Israelite king himself, seemed extrapolated. The capital of a stone column that had been unearthed was affixed with a label reading, in part, "many of the City of David's secrets remain hidden in the ground," as though to imply great secrets and discoveries to come. After my self-guided tour, I sat in on a 3D film that featured a man dressed in the manner of Indiana Jones narrating an animated reenactment of the conquest of the City of Jerusalem by David's army. At the end of the film the man declared, with a hint of triumph, that the original rulers of the land had at last returned. This return could be celebrated in a variety of ways. Whatever it lacked in science, the City of David made up for in merriment. The site offered a "Hallelujah night show" and the promise of a "magical, mysterious journey to the heart of Jerusalem." Future plans included a cable car and a zip line.

I now understood what Nasser meant by a "tourist center dedicated to biblical times." And I recognized the fragile triumphalism here, the desperate need to assert royal lineage and great ancestral deeds. And I could not help but wonder if this triumphalism was born out of refutation—out of a need to prove that one's people are not "animals" who have "ruined every country they ever entered." I'd seen it all my life in the invocations of great kingdoms and ancient empires—a search for provenance and noble roots. It was the oddest thing—the conqueror still conquered by Niggerology. And now Zionism had moved into a dark third act wherein noble roots must yield noble privilege.

A day earlier, I toured a settlement and saw something that appeared drawn from the world of Mad Max. At the boundary of this settlement, every thirty feet or so, I would see a guard dog rise, growl, and loudly bark. I looked closer and saw a leash attached to each of these dogs. The leashes extended perhaps ten feet up, where they met, at a perpendicular angle, a master cord stretched across the space. The effect was a kind of fencing, a wall made of guard dogs. I felt myself in the presence of a terrible chimera—a wall of hell hounds that seemed to me drawn from my Montgomery nightmares.

There was something insecure about that chimera too, about whoever had engineered it. To construct what amounts to a wall of devouring, you must be *really* afraid of something. Maybe that's what happens when annihilation is no longer speculative but a fact of national and personal history. That's the easy answer. The more disturbing one is that this wall represented nothing new, that it was no more spectacular than the rituals of lynching, that the mob too was insecure, that its rituals too spoke to white men's violent impotence. And oddly enough, I had the same feeling as I left the City of David—that I was in the presence of a violent impotence. It all felt so fake. And beholding the redemption of Eretz Israel, the ostensible homecoming of an ancient people, announced in 3D projection and accessed via zip line, I could not escape the feeling of being in the presence of a poorly wrought fairy tale and an enormous con. I was in the land that Uris so adored, where the New Jew "spits in the eye of the Arab hordes." But the very violence and force that emanated even from the City of David spoke to the disquiet and fear that resided somewhere deep inside Israel. The state doth protest too much. It occurred to me that if Jewish national honor had indeed been redeemed, the Israelis themselves did not quite believe it.

We left the complex and walked toward the Old City proper. To the west I could see a number of buildings rising on the hillside. Some of these buildings had eyes painted on them, peering down on the City of David. In the Old City we met Alon Arad, an archaeologist at Tel Aviv University, and Amy Cohen, a local housing activist. If this strikes you as an odd combination, you are forgiven—it struck me the same way. I had given some acquaintances a rough outline of my interests, and they'd pulled together a list of people I should see and in what order. I gave myself over to that list without question—it's not like I had any basis to disagree. That was how I came to the City of David. It was recommended that I see this "archaeological amusement park" alone first, and then tour both the Old City and the City of David again in the company of professionals.

It was sage advice. This was the second time I visited the Old City. Previously, I had entered as a Muslim, through the Lion's Gate, and my guides were Muslim or Arab, which reduced my access but expanded my understanding of the city's invisible borders. Now, I came through the Jaffa Gate—the way most foreign, non-Muslim tourists arrive. The difference was palpable, and as in Tel Aviv, as I wended my way through a crush of happy tourists and crossed through joyous bar mitzvah parties, I felt as though I were in another country.

After lunch, we walked back out through the Jaffa Gate and approached a tunnel guarded by a checkpoint. The guards looked at my passport and eyed me warily before letting us pass. After we were through, Amy explained that Palestinians were generally turned away at that checkpoint. After the checkpoint, we reached a plaza, and from a distance I saw a line of worshippers standing before the Western Wall, believed to date back to the time of Herod some two thousand years ago, which borders the Temple Mount. Looking out on the plaza, filled with worshippers and tourists, I understood that I was standing in a place meant to inspire reverence and solemnity. But by then I knew how easily such feelings could be transformed into a casus belli. And I also knew, by then, that the Western Wall as I now saw it, with its sprawling plaza, evidenced that transformation.

In 1967, when the IDF conquered East Jerusalem and the Old City, Israel rejoiced. "We have returned to the holiest of our places," General Moshe Dayan told

Life magazine. "Never to depart from it again." No place was more holy than the Western Wall, that relic of an era when the Jewish kings of old ruled over the Old City. For centuries, Jewish worshippers had negotiated their rights to pray at the Western Wall with the Muslim rulers of Jerusalem, who venerated Aqsa, which abutted the Wall. Jerusalem's new rulers imagined a broad plaza where the faithful could worship en masse. But there was a familiar problem—someone was already there. In 1193, Malik Al-Afdal, son of Saladin, scourge of the Crusaders, deeded a parcel of land in front of the Wall to worshippers and Islamic scholars from North Africa or the Maghreb.

By the time Dayan arrived in the Old City, the eight-hundred-year-old Moroccan Quarter, as it came to be known, was housing 108 families living on roughly three city blocks. Journalist Abdallah Schleifer described the quarter as "a pleasant and architecturally distinct quarter of freshly whitewashed roof terraces, gardens, and neat unattached houses built in North African style several hundred years ago to house Moroccan soldiers garrisoning Jerusalem for the Ottomans." This description stood in sharp contrast with that of Zionist leader Chaim Weizmann, who, in an appeal to Lord Balfour for custody of the Quarter, described it as a collection of "miserable cottages and derelict buildings." Weizmann offered to purchase the Quarter but was rebuffed, as all subsequent efforts were. But what could not be bought could be captured by the sword. "The day after the Old City fell," wrote Teddy Kollek, then mayor of Jerusalem, "it also became clear to me that something had to be done about the small slum houses that crowded close to the Western Wall."

As early as 1887, Baron Edmond de Rothschild had proposed purchasing and leveling the quarter to create a plaza for worshippers. Three days after the Old City fell, Rothschild's vision quickly became a reality when Israeli bulldozers razed the quarter. One hundred thirty-five homes were demolished and 650 people rendered homeless. At least one woman was crushed after remaining inside her home. "People felt depressed because these houses weren't just their property, but also the property of their ancestors, from 800 years ago—or more," a resident later remembered. "They told us to take everything as fast as possible because we didn't have time. . . . Some people took their stuff like crazies and just stormed out of their houses. In an unbelievable way. It was 'quick, quick—haul your things and get out, yalla, quickly quickly.' . . . They didn't let anyone stay. They emptied the entire neighborhood in a heartbeat."

The nominal reason for destroying the Moroccan Quarter was want of space for Jewish worshippers. But just as the Zionists sought to bolster their own title deed, the annihilation of the Moroccan Quarter allowed for the destruction of any competing claim. There was a brute literalism to this process, a direct connection between the murky, symbolic claims of ancestry and the very real and exclusive claims being made on Palestinian land. And that process is ongoing. The City of David presents its aims as educational—connecting people, through a mix of archaeology and tourism, with the Jewish past. In fact, its designs are deeper. It is run by a private settler organization that was given custody of the dig site by the state. Our visit took place on the eighth day of my trip, and by then I knew enough to understand that the prime purpose of any "settler organization" was to push Palestinians out and to move Jewish Israelis in.

One method of effecting this was to declare a piece of land to be an archaeological site, thus allowing the state to assert an interest in how that site is used. In Area C, where Nasser and all Palestinians are subject to Israeli rule, state interests can mean outright eviction. Here in East Jerusalem, where Palestinians have "residency"— not citizenship—eviction is more complicated. So while the state declaring your home an archaeological site may not lead to outright eviction, it does allow for excavation in front of—or tunneling directly beneath—your home. And in the case of the City of David, it also allows for flooding your neighborhood with tourists hopped up on tales of religious jingoism, primed to regard you as an occupier of their God-given land. The aim, Alon explained, was to create a "correlation between Jewish heritage and ownership" and to birth a generation who could not imagine anything other than complete Jewish rule over Eretz Israel. As I stood there watching the worshippers, Alon pointed to what appeared to be the ruins of an ancient wall. Standing there, amid all that remained of the Moroccan Quarter, amid a lost world, I felt a mix of astonishment, betrayal, and anger. The astonishment was for me—for my own ignorance, for my own incuriosity, for the limits of my sense of reparations. The betrayal was for my colleagues in journalism—betrayal for the way they reported, for the way they'd laundered open discrimination, for the voices they'd erased. And the anger was for my own past—for Black Bottom, for Rosewood, for Tulsa—which I could not help but feel being evoked here.

When we walked back out, away from the ghosts of the Mughrabi Quarter, we headed back to the City of

David. On this second trip I noticed something that I had missed the first time: that just a short walk from the main dig was a small residential neighborhood with houses lining one side of the street. Some of those homes flew Israeli flags and some didn't. This was still East Jerusalem—occupied territory. The Israeli flags proudly announced that this territory was being actively colonized. And thinking back on Alon's explanation, I understood that this space had a story that was not inert or ancient; it was alive, and it was being used to promote what I could now see as a slow but constant ethnic cleanse.

Everywhere I went that week, in the Occupied Territories, in East Jerusalem, in Haifa, and in the stories told by Palestinians and even by Israelis, I felt that the state had one message to the Palestinians within its borders. The message was: "You'd really be better off somewhere else." Sometimes, the message was conveyed brutally, as when Nasser and his family were driven out of their home. But here in Jerusalem, the tactics were more subtle. The City of David simply made it extremely uncomfortable for Palestinians to be here. I thought back to my visit to Columbia, South Carolina, and all the monuments to the enslavers and advocates of Jim Crow. I thought of how the Confederate flag had once flown over the State House. I thought of the kind of people who came to see those monuments, who thought the flag to be important. And then I imagined the state that ruled over me and my family importing all of that to my very front door.

And what I was seeing here seemed about as credible as the history behind those Confederate memorials. The City of David employed a sheen of ancient provenance and archaeological science, but it was still unclear to me whether this had ever been a city or had ever been ruled by a king named David.

"Is this the City of David?" I asked Alon.

"It is an Iron Age city from two hundred years later than King David's reign," he said.

"So he's basically dead by the time this—"

Alon interrupted, "I don't think he ever lived."

He said this in the matter-of-fact way befitting his profession—swatting away the kind of myth a layperson would take as history. Archaeology was interpretive, Alon explained. You find four walls, and you call it a room—and if you are predisposed to believe that you are in the seat of an ancient kingdom, then why can't it be the throne room? We walked on until we reached an outdoor welcoming area, where Alon pointed me toward a plaque engraved in the wall. The plaque bore the flag of the United States and the name of one of its former ambassadors to Israel. I moved closer to read the inscription: "The City of David brings Biblical Jerusalem to life at the very place where the kings and the prophets of the Bible walked," read the plaque. "The spiritual bedrock of our values as a nation comes from Jerusalem. It is upon these ideals that the American republic was founded, and the unbreakable bond between the United States and Israel was formed."

Here Alon abandoned his clinical disposition and raised his voice. The City of David "managed to get so mainstream that the American ambassador comes here and declares that this place is part of the glorious heritage of the United States of America abroad," he said. "Now there is an American heritage abroad. It's usually cemeteries in Normandy. Yeah, that's American heritage abroad. City of David is not. And when you talk about white supremacy and when you talk about how things look here, this is why I think that the Evangelical church and the settlers found each other as a perfect match. Their mindset is the same. They do other things, but their mindset is the same—"

I interrupted Alon: "I gotta take a second. Let me just sit down."

I walked away and found a seat in the shade, away

from everyone. At this moment, all that I had seen across the days began to avalanche—the cave evictions, the massacre in Hebron, the monuments to genocide, the checkpoints, the wall of devouring, and so much more. Those who question Israel, who question what has been done with the moral badge of the Holocaust, are often pointed in the direction of the great evils done across the world. We are told that it is suspicious that, among all the ostensibly amoral states, we would single out Israel—as though the relationship between America and Israel is not itself singular. But the plaque was clear: "The spiritual bedrock of our values as a nation come from Jerusalem." This effort that I saw, the use of archaeology, the destruction of ancient sites, the pushing of Palestinians out of their homes, had the specific imprimatur of the United States of America. Which means that it had my imprimatur. This was not just another evil done by another state, but an evil done in my name.

We left the City of David and descended into a valley where more excavation was in process—a search for the ancient Pool of Siloam where, it is said, Jesus once healed the blind. In search of the pool, the City of David, along with the Israeli government, seized and destroyed the orchard of a Palestinian family. Evidence of the pool's existence and miraculous powers had yet to emerge. But to focus on the facts of the story is to miss the whole point of the City of David. As one of its officials told a reporter, the tourists here are "looking to hear some nice stories. They don't want to go to a lecture from some professor." Pressed on the historical accuracy of the City of David's very name, the official was unmoved. "We've yet to find a sign saying 'Welcome to King David's palace.' Maybe that will be discovered, maybe not."

I got back to the hotel that afternoon exhausted as usual—so exhausted, in fact, that I didn't even see the man standing at the hotel's front door. Or maybe I did see him and did not quite register his role until he blocked my path. "Are you a guest here?" he asked. He addressed me with a kind of well-mannered hostility— like an English inspector who keeps calling his suspect "sir." I was fixated on the gun holstered on his hip. I reached into my pocket, flashed my key card, and walked inside. I moved through the lobby, shook, and got to my room as fast as I could.

I don't think I ever, in my life, felt the glare of racism burn stranger and more intense than in Israel. There

are aspects I found familiar—the light-skinned Palestinians who speak of "passing," the Black and Arab Jews
whose stories could have been staged in Atlanta instead
of Tel Aviv. But for most of my time there, I felt like I
was outside the crosshairs. The attitude in that hotel, for
instance, was less "Nigger get out" and more "What the
fuck are you doing here?" They were right. The hotel
was very nice. But knowing how it had been gotten,
knowing how it was secured, knowing the gigantic
Dream that had drawn most of its guests, and knowing
how I had imagined that there could be some break
from it all, some comfort amid an active ethnic cleanse,
an active colonization, I could only ask myself, What
the fuck am I doing here?

In some sense, my trip to the Land of Palestine was
a journey backward toward that instinct I'd lost, an ancestral gift I'd forgotten. The gift is not in the blood but
in the stories, the axioms, the experiences garnered
from centuries of living on the outskirts of a dubious
democracy. When I went off to become a professional
writer, I was brimming with my own skepticism—not
of the country but of the gift, which seemed so diffuse
and random, a kind of folk wisdom that stood in abeyance of the empirical. Perhaps the most important fact

in this skepticism was that I had no living models. The few Black writers working at the journals and magazines I read seemed bent on putting as much distance between themselves and Black people as possible. That wasn't me. If I was skeptical of the gift, I was never skeptical of the people. I came to think of my trade—long-form magazine or new journalism—as a kind of scientific process that, when correctly applied, must necessarily reveal the truth. And for a time I saw the practitioner of that science as an individual, as singular, as standing alone, applying the process, searching for truth. And then I found myself in newsrooms where, for the first time in my life, I was often an only, in newsrooms with no Black editors. I thought I could stand apart, but looking back, I see that the parts of my thinking that were most reinforced were those that most dovetailed with those around me, and the parts that were hardest to hold were those that did not. I wrote a lot of stuff I came to regret—a lot of smart-ass contrarianism, a lot of mean prose—in the young rush to get into the paper or magazine. And even after I matured, I found that my old instincts had not. I became a better technical writer, but my sense of the world was stunted. There were no Palestinian writers or editors around me. But there were many writers, editors, and publishers who believed in the nobility of Zionism and had little regard for, or simply could not see, its victims.

Zionism's victims. Even now, after all I have seen, my pen skips as I write this to you. I'm back in New York, sipping my morning coffee, Joan Armatrading in the background— *"Are you for or against us, we are trying to get somewhere"*—and just as over there, a beautiful sun is hanging in a cloudless sky. I've been home for a year, but sometimes I still dream that I am back in Palestine. Some of those dreams are pleasant—I am at peace on a cliff in Sakiya, I am folding green falafel into warm ka'ak al qud, I am feeling the crush and energy of Ramallah, I am smiling at a little girl in Tuba who wants to practice her English. So my pen skips here, as it should, because to be Palestinian is to be more than a victim of Zionism. And there's something else.

Zionism was conceived as a counter to an oppression that feels very familiar. I read the early Zionist Moses Hess naming himself as part of "an unfortunate, maligned, despised, and dispersed people—but one that the world has not succeeded in destroying," and I hear the prophets of Black nationalism, the struggle into which I was born, the struggle of Garvey and Malcolm, the struggle that gave me my very name. "Jewish noses cannot be reformed," Hess told his people. "And the black, wavy hair of the Jews will not be changed into blond by conversion or straightened out by constant combing." Addressing the efforts of German Jews to integrate, Hess was skeptical:

> You may mask yourself a thousand times over; you may change your name, religion, and character; you may travel through the world incognito, so that people may not recognize the Jew in you; yet every insult to the Jewish name will strike you even more than the honest man who admits his Jewish loyalties and who fights for the honor of the Jewish name.

That last part, "the honor of the Jewish name," I knew well. So much of what I saw during those ten days seemed explicitly about that particular mission. Honor. Even the platitude "Israel has the right to defend itself" made sense in the context of a people who'd so often been made to dance for their killers. "Stupid is the person who believes in his neighbor," Jabotinsky warned,

> good and loving as the neighbor may be; stupid is the person who relies on justice. Justice exists

only for those whose fists and stubbornness make it possible for them to realize it. . . . Do not believe anyone, be always on guard, carry your stick always with you—this is the only way of surviving in this wolfish battle of all against all.

That was 1911. Within forty years, the West would stand by and watch as a third of the Jewish people were consumed. I think of the fury the Shoah's survivors must have felt, the rage at their oppressors, at the bystanders, and then, finally, at the humanistic impulse that made them think anyone else would ever care. I see myself in that fury when my battered people are told to turn the other cheek. I see myself in Moses Hess inveighing against the "mask" of passing.

Israel felt like an alternative history, one where all our Garvey dreams were made manifest. There, "Up Ye Mighty Race" was the creed. There, "Redemption Song" is the national anthem. There, the red black and green billowed over schools, embassies, and the columns of great armies. There, Martin Delaney is a hero and February 21 is a day of mourning. That was the dream— the mythic Africa my father cannot get back to. I think it's best that way—for should that mythic Africa have ever descended out of the imagination and into the real, I shudder at what we might lose in realizing and defending it.

What I saw in the City of David was so familiar to me—the search for self in an epic, mythic past filled with kings and sanctified by an approximation of science. Perhaps, then, it is unsurprising that as I saw something familiar in Zionism, Zionism saw something familiar in me. "There is still one other question arising out of the disaster of nations which remains unsolved to this day, and whose profound tragedy, only a Jew can comprehend," wrote Herzl.

This is the African question. Just call to mind all those terrible episodes of the slave trade, of human beings who, merely because they were black, were stolen like cattle, taken prisoner, captured and sold. Their children grew up in strange lands, the objects of contempt and hostility because their complexions were different. I am not ashamed to say, though I may expose myself to ridicule for saying so, that once I have witnessed the redemption of the Jews, my people, I wish also to assist in the redemption of the Africans.

Herzl was not alone. Golda Meir fashioned ties with newly liberated African states and loudly denounced apartheid. In 1964, while visiting Victoria Falls on the Zambian side, Meir, as foreign minister, was invited across the border to Rhodesia (today Zimbabwe) by its white supremacist rulers. Meir refused. By all accounts, she sincerely believed that racism against Black Africans was wrong. Still, there were always those who saw in Meir and her country something less than egalitarian. "They took Israel away from the Arabs after the Arabs lived there for a thousand years," said South African prime minister Hendrik Verwoerd in 1961. "In that, I agree with them. Israel, like South Africa, is an apartheid state."

The charge of Israeli apartheid has long been rejected by Zionists as antithetical to the very nature of a Jewish state infused with the traumas of its people. The special nature of Israel's mission as antiracist flows through the words of its own leaders, from David Ben-Gurion ("A Jew can't be for discrimination") to Shimon Peres ("A Jew who accepts apartheid ceases to be a Jew") to Benjamin Netanyahu ("For the Jewish people, apartheid is the ultimate abomination. It is an expression of the cruelest inhumanity. Israel will do everything possible to eliminate this odious system"). But this rhetoric cannot stand against the record.

In 1974, with Meir now prime minister, *Haaretz* began mining the darkest depths of white racism—publishing a caricature of cannibalistic African leaders devouring Israeli politicians, while Meir danced with an African man. That same year, Meir—once horrified by white racism in Africa—dispatched defense minister Shimon Peres to Pretoria. On his return to Tel Aviv, Peres thanked his host, stressing that "the new links which you have helped to forge between our two countries will develop into a close identity of aspirations and interests which will turn out to be of long-standing benefit to both our countries."

That is exactly what happened. Israeli officials opened a lucrative arms trade with South Africa, upgraded South Africa's air force, and held an annual joint intelligence conference. South African officials hosted their Israeli counterparts on safaris, enjoyed Israeli support for their dubious "Bantustan" policy, and kept an open dialogue on the best practices by which one might best divorce a people from its various freedoms. In 1977, South African Army chief Constand Viljoen marveled at the efficiency of the Israeli checkpoints in the Occupied Territories. "The thoroughness with which Israel conducts this examination is astonishing," Viljoen noted. "At the quickest, it takes individual Arabs that come through there about one and a half hours. When the traffic is heavy, it takes from four to five hours."

By the time Menachem Begin took office in the late 1970s, no single country was buying more Israeli arms than South Africa. The money for those guns was plundered from Black South Africans deprived of their rights and then used to fund a Zionist order that subsequently deprived Palestinians of theirs. When Israel was finally pressured into publicly severing ties with South Africa in the mid-1980s, its national security establishment was apoplectic. "A change in the security export policy will mean the firing of tens of thousands of workers," warned Defense Minister Yitzhak Rabin. "I hereby inform you that they will not find an alternative opportunity."

Quietly, Israel agreed. While publicly distancing itself from South Africa, Israel continued trading, right up until the fall of apartheid. Among the last conversations: the production and employment of chemical and biological weapons. All told, from 1974 to 1993, total annual exports from Tel Aviv to Pretoria averaged $600 million a year. Through all those critical years, Israel was not just an ally of South Africa; it was the very arsenal of apartheid.

This partnership was a matter not strictly of real-politik but of a genuine affinity. During World War II, the Afrikaner politician John Vorster lobbied for his country to enter the war on the side of Nazi Germany, despite South Africa's historical ties to the United Kingdom. "We stand for Christian Nationalism, which is an ally of National Socialism," Vorster said. "In Italy it is called Fascism, in Germany National Socialism, and in South Africa Christian Nationalism." But by 1976, Vorster was the prime minister of South Africa—a state with deep ties to Israel. That year he was received as a guest at that indelible site of Jewish pain and mourning, Yad Vashem.

There were dissidents in Israel who saw in this reception a betrayal of Zionism. Arthur Goldreich had fought in the 1948 war that brought Israel into existence. But as a South African Jew, he well knew the evil that Vorster represented. Goldreich began hanging posters on telephone poles equating Vorster with Nazism, in protest of the prime minister's visit. His protest was interrupted by an elderly man who had an Auschwitz tattoo. Goldreich thought that the man would sympathize with him. Instead, he spat on the poster and said, "We will make agreements with the devil to save Jews from persecution and to secure the future of this state."

But the security of Israel did not just require an agreement with apartheid—it required that Israel practice apartheid itself. Israel's defenders claim that the apartheid charge, like the charge of colonialism, is little more than ad hominem seeking to undermine that last redoubt of the Jewish people. Human rights groups disagree and point to the definition enshrined in international law, which defines the crime of apartheid as "inhuman acts committed for the purpose of establishing and maintaining domination by one racial group of persons over any other racial group of persons and systematically oppressing them."

This definition matched everything I saw on the ground during my trip. Perhaps more importantly, Israel's own leaders have long seen apartheid as well within the range of possibilities for its government. In 2007, Israeli prime minister Ehud Olmert warned that without a "two-state solution" Israel would "face a South African–style struggle for equal voting rights." The result of that struggle in Olmert's mind would be grim— "the state of Israel [would be] finished." Three years later, Ehud Barak, then serving as Netanyahu's defense minister, issued a warning:

As long as in this territory west of the Jordan river there is only one political entity called Israel it is going to be either non-Jewish, or non-democratic. If this bloc of millions of Palestinians cannot vote, that will be an apartheid state.

I think back to my visit to Yad Vashem, and I think back to sitting there, contemplating the Book of Names. I think of myself standing before the conveyor belt of time. And I think of John Vorster in that same space. I see him laying a wreath bearing the colors of his country before a memorial to the victims of the Shoah. And I see the literal standard of white supremacy taking its place at a monument to some six million of its victims.

The link is colonialism, which has always had a racist cynicism at its core—a belief that the world is not just savage, but that the most dangerous savages tend to live beyond the borders of the West. Zionism—which from the outset sought to position itself as "an outpost of civilization against barbarism"—has never rejected these precepts. The Israeli historian Benny Morris has been celebrated for his willingness to see Zionism's history with clarity and candor. Would that he could bring that same clarity to Zionism's victims. In a 2004 interview with *Hadretz,* Morris described Palestinians as "barbarians who want to take our lives." There was but one way to constrain the threat: "Something like a cage has to be built for them. . . . There is a wild animal there that has to be locked up in one way or another." Pushed to reflect on the fate of those to be "locked up," Morris could barely muster a shrug. Instead, Morris approvingly invoked a genocide. "Even the great American democracy could not have been created without the annihilation of the Indians."

I'm not sure when, exactly, during my visit I first heard the term *the Naqba.* Perhaps it was after being held at bay at the Lion's Gate. Perhaps it was while touring the neighborhood of Sheikh Jarrah in East Jerusalem, where I saw the bulk trash that settlers from Long Island had tossed into the yards of Palestinian families. The phrase, which means "the catastrophe," originates in the driving of some seven hundred thousand Palestinians from their homes in 1948 and continues in the perpetual process of ethnic cleansing I saw in my ten days. By the end of my visit, I understood the Naqba as a particular thing, ranging even beyond any analogies with Jim Crow, colonialism, or apartheid. It is not just the cops shooting your son, though there is that too. It is not just a racist carceral project, though that is here too.

And it is not just an inequality before the law, though that was everywhere I looked. It is the thing that each of those devices served—a plunder of your home, a plunder both near and perpetual:

We live, if we are able to live, in an infant past, planted in fields that were ours for hundreds of years until a moment ago, before the dough rose and coffeepots cooled . . .

The discordance in Mahmoud Darwish's words—fields planted and plowed for centuries whose loss is measured in hours, even minutes—makes the pain of his agony glow. I read these words and see a theft that is at once old and in progress. But, too, I see the intimacy of a loss—the neighbors vanquished and the flags of the vanquisher a short walk away. "What wounds you most," writes Darwish, "is that 'there' is so close to 'here.'"

On April 9, 1948, as Zionist militias fought to establish a Jewish state, they closed in on the small village of Deir Yassin. The advance was led by the Irgun and their off-shoot Lehi—two Zionist militias notorious for murdering civilians. The Lehi were openly racist, describing Jews as a "master race" and Arabs as a "slave race." Setting up outside Deir Yassin, they battled the village's Palestinian defenders throughout the day and, after taking the town, slaughtered at least a hundred inhabitants. The news of the massacre quickly swept across Palestinian communities and greatly aided the efforts of the advancing Zionist militias to purge the land of Arabs and build a "Jewish democracy." I didn't find out about Deir Yassin until I was back in America, but I likely drove past it several times. The remnants of the village are in Jerusalem, just a short drive from Yad Vashem.

The proximity of the two sites staggered me. I called Sam Bahour, a Palestinian-American friend I'd made in Ramallah, and vented my surprise. "They do this all the time," he said. He told me about the Museum of Tolerance in Jerusalem—another site of memory, this one built directly on top of a Muslim graveyard. Sam had not once exaggerated or steered me wrong about Palestine. And when he told me about the Museum of Tolerance, I knew it was true, but part of me just could not accept it. But a few clicks into a search engine proved him right. Again, my own disbelief was the hope of a way out of that yawning darkness I first glimpsed in Yad

Vashem. A museum dedicated to "tolerance" literally
built on the grave of the occupied annuls that hope. But
in the darkness, there is light.

In the first weeks after I returned from Palestine, I
held Yad Vashem at a distance from Israel itself—its
echoes to white supremacy, colonial roots, its apartheid
policies. This distance served me. It allowed me to hold
onto something pure in suffering. I knew that some Zionists invoked the Holocaust to justify their repression
of Palestinians. And I had seen Ben-Gurion at the end
of the Hall of Remembrance. But even after all I'd seen,
I craved my own arc, my own circle, a story of perfect
geometry. And then I learned about Vorster's visit, and
that a memorial to genocide was built within walking
distance of a massacre that had made that memorial possible, and the arc bent and the circle broke.

I found myself obsessing over everything I had
missed in Palestine. I thought of all the things I'd caught
glimpses of but had not really understood in enough
detail to write about. And this combined with something surprising—a genuine longing for Palestine, not
just as a reporter but as a human. I thought of that in
Sakiya, unlike anything I've ever felt. I thought of walking the streets of Ramallah with the great journalist
Amira Hass. I thought of Ali Awad in Tuba. I thought

of Batan Al-Hawa, the eyes painted on the homes in the hills and how they looked right out on the City of David. I thought of Tania Nasr, who on the last night of the festival sang for us all. I went to see her days later. Then she told me of her life—growing up in Ramallah and spending time in Jaffa, where her family had been driven from. She brewed Arabic coffee, served a kind of cookie with dates in the middle, and then conjured a lost world:

> I was the first grandchild in the family. So my aunts would take me to the beach. I have photographs, I'll show you now. I remember walking on the sand looking for small crabs on the rocks. I remember picking up shells. And my aunts would make them into necklaces for me. They would call me the Little Hawaiian, put little skirts on me and whatnot. But when I went back to the beach, I broke up. It's the water, I think.

What I knew then was that these ten days, these words I write, were a beginning, not an end. And what was also clear was that I had gone to Palestine, like I'd gone to Senegal, in pursuit of my own questions, and thus had not fully seen the people on their own terms.

Perhaps that's why I kept thinking of Deir Yassin. I spent so much time considering the force and import of Yad Vashem, and did so with no knowledge of that massacre so close to this site of mourning. I felt that I was still waking up, feel that I am still waking up, still searching for the right words, still trying to see a people whose oppression depended on their erasure. And I could not end this story there.

When I was working on "The Case for Reparations," it was important to me that it not merely be a technical or historical argument but that the living speak for themselves, that the plunder which I inveighed against be understood as more than a dead relic of the past. The point was to draw the reader in as close proximity to the crime as possible, to reach through the haze of years and clarify with the words of those who bore witness. But there was something else—my own deep need to hear those words for myself, to know for myself what I had come to suspect through books, papers, and reports. And I felt that same need again with this act of reparation—the need to hear for myself.

And so through a string of Palestinian contacts I reached ninety-one-year-old Hassan Jaber, who was thirteen years old when the Lehi and Irgun militias set upon his home of Deir Yassin. Mr. Jaber—this is what I feel comfortable calling him—lived in America, I was told, and he would talk to me in person at his home, in the town of Orland Park, just outside of Chicago. I had to go. I was still thinking of Yad Vashem and all that I had borne witness to. And after hearing about Deir Yassin, I thought that I had not borne witness to the fullness of it all, that the story had ended in too easy a place—one that was convenient for the state project I now believed Yad Vashem served. And I was thinking of Clyde Ross, Mattie Lewis, and Ethel Weatherspoon. It had been ten years since I'd flown to Chicago to see them—survivors of a different demographic project—whose words became the spine of "The Case for Reparations."

My wife and I flew in to see Mr. Jaber one afternoon in May. But our first stop was to the home of Dina Elmuti-Hasan, who'd connected us with Mr. Jaber. Dina's grandmother, Fatima Radwan, had also survived the massacre of Deir Yassin, and Dina had spent years recording her grandmother's stories. Dina and her husband, Gaith, welcomed us into their home. They served us coffee and warm knafeh—the traditional Middle Eastern dessert of pastry, cheese, and syrup. Their five-year-old son gave us a tour of his impressive collection of Lego models—spacecraft, the Empire State Building, Al-Aqsa. They talked of their different familial pathways out of Palestine and into America, and the maze of regulations that must be negotiated to go back for visits. All the details of the visit mattered to me, because I no longer trusted the picture conjured by the word "Palestinian" as projected from America's most trusted news sources. It is painful to admit to that, because I'm part of it, because I believed in it, and because I think the questioning, for me, has only just begun.

Mr. Jaber's home was a five-minute drive away. His granddaughter Saswan, who'd agreed to translate, greeted us at the door. Her skin was a deep brown. She smiled as we approached from the car, but when she spoke there was a force in her voice that was familiar—like my old middle school teachers who knew that a large part of their job was letting you know that they did not play. We walked in and there was Mr. Jaber—spry and smiling, in glasses and a blue gingham shirt. He walked us into the living room and we sat there and listened as he unspooled his life for us. He recalled the Deir Yassin of before, the produce—the figs, plums, grapes, and apples—and his people's strong connection to the land, a connection he kept through the gardens outside his home. He recalled his six sisters and five brothers, his father, who'd passed away before the battle, and his mother, Jamilah, a widow, who on that morning went off with the men to defend the town. Saswan pulled up a picture from her phone—it was Jamilah, her great-grandmother, in a white hijab, behind earthworks, with a rifle.

It was important to him that I understand the odds they faced—that they were outnumbered and out-gunned, that they fought until their last bullet. It was important to him that I understand that his brother had been blindfolded and shot execution-style. He told me that he was too young to fight, and when the battle seemed lost, he was charged with carrying his sisters, aged three and five, out of the village to safety. It never occurred to Mr. Jaber, or any who survived Deir Yassin, that this was the beginning of an exodus, that a new state—one that defined them out of it—would be built on their homes. He said, "We never expected that we would go seventy-six years leaving there and we cannot go back. . . . Seventy-six years now."

Those seventy-six years took Mr. Jaber across the map of the Middle East and the Americas—Ein Karim, Jerusalem, Jericho, Brazil, back to Jerusalem, Puerto Rico, and then to America. He built a family and a suc-cessful business trading gold and silver. He now has 150 children, grandchildren, and great-grandchildren, and to them he passed down his stories and a strong sense that they be remembered. "I think about my entire childhood," Saswan said. "He would sit us all down, all his grandkids, and keep telling us that our liberation was through our education and that we couldn't forget. Because when Palestine was colonized, what they said was they'll grow old and their children will forget."

We said our goodbyes to Mr. Jaber and then followed Saswan in her car to a Middle-Eastern restaurant a few miles away in nearby Chicagoland for a gathering of friends and fellow Palestinian activists, teachers, and lawyers. We ordered fatoush, yalanji, kubbeh, and hummus. A man in a keffiyeh kept coming by serving Arabic coffee—the kind I'd had at Tania's home in Birzeit. Every thirty minutes or so, the volume of the music would rise and there'd be a huge sing-along for someone's birthday or some other celebratory occasion. Saswan kept apologizing for the festivities. But the food, the volume of song, the coffee, the whole day, all of it combined to impart a feeling of coming back to a home, even though it was not my own. I had not made it back to Palestine, but I had found something this day that I hadn't even found over there. In Palestine I was always being guided, speaking or visiting through intermediaries. But here, I felt something that I have always enjoyed about reporting, about seeing worlds beyond my own—I feel myself disappear. When no one is holding my hand or guiding me, and I am watching people living out their particular customs, engaged in their small conversations, I can feel myself dissolving into it all.

The group spoke about politics in a manner of communal intimacy—the way my people speak when no white people are around. For that reason alone, I would rather not tell you their names. But when I asked to write about this moment, they were insistent that they, as Palestinians, had been made nameless for too long. They were Deanna Othman, Noor Ali, and Tarek Khalil. Tarek explained the maddening inconsistencies of Israeli law. Deanna's husband was from Gaza and she explained the great difficulty of trekking through Egypt and through the Rafah crossing to enter Gaza and visit her family. Deanna told me she now taught at a school where most of the kids were Palestinian, and she loved teaching "The Case for Reparations." She said, "The kids always say, Yeah, but about the Israel part? And I just say, Well, nobody's perfect." I could only laugh.

We would talk more later, and I would learn that, in addition to teaching, Deanna was a journalist herself—

a graduate of Medill, one of the most well-regarded journalism schools in the country. She left Medill with all the hopes and dreams that her summa cum laude status would normally inspire, but what she found was that it was impossible to make a career as a Palestinian journalist who held Palestine close to her. She understood journalism, and writing, as I did—as a way of drawing the boundaries of the world. At Medill, she'd dreamed of drawing those brackets from the perspective of a Palestinian woman. It was a perspective that, in all my time in journalism, in all the newsrooms in which I'd worked, in the journalism schools where I had taught, I had never once encountered. She spoke about the impossibility of finding work that allowed her to write as she wished, and I could tell by the way she spoke that this frustrated dream was not just hers but one she held for her people, for she too was a steward, and she too was a bearer, and she too had ancestors.

We know what this is, you and I. Writing is a powerful tool of politics. Harriet Jacobs exposed the violence and rape at the root of chattel slavery. Ida B. Wells's reportage dispelled the grotesque myths of monstrous Black masculinity that undergirded lynching. W.E.B. Du Bois debunked the Confederate hagiography historians employed to justify driving Black people from the polls. This has happened despite a concerted effort to deny Black writers access to leading journals and publishers, to assault their schools and libraries, to outlaw reading and writing itself, and thus deny their access to this tool which is not just powerful but nonviolent. This is important—forced to match sword for sword, or gun for gun, slaveholders and white supremacists could be confident in victory, if only because their vast wealth assured them an unmatched arsenal. But the rules of writing are different, and great wealth has almost the same relationship to creating great writers as it does great basketball players. A literature fueled by a profound human experience must necessarily burn at a high flame, and thus a "material handicap" is transformed into a "spiritual advantage," putting in the hands of the oppressed "the conditions of a classical art," which is to say the power to haunt people, to move people, and expand the brackets of humanity. This is as true for those laboring under the shadow of enslavement as it is for those laboring under the shadow of apartheid.

But that power needs a host, as sure as an arrow needs a longbow to launch it. It is no mistake that my own rise in the world of journalism directly coincided with employment at the most well-resourced magazine I'd worked for in my life. American journalism has rarely lavished such resources on Palestinian writers—indeed, it seems largely disinterested in what they have to say. In 2020, the historian Maha Nassar surveyed the nation's opinion pages and journals to see how often Palestinian writers were granted access. What she found was that the country's papers and magazines preferred writing about Palestinians to allowing Palestinians to write. Through a fifty-year period stretching from 1970 to 2019, Nassar found that less than 2 percent of all opinion pieces discussing Palestinians had Palestinian authors. *The Washington Post* ranked at a dismal 1 percent. *The New Republic* during this period did not publish a single piece on Palestine from the perspective of Palestinians.

I do not believe that this is a conspiracy. But more important, I do not think it is a coincidence. An inhumane system demands inhumans, and so it produces them in stories, editorials, newscasts, movies, and television. Editors and writers like to think they are not part of such systems, that they are independent, objective, and arrive at their conclusions solely by dint of their reporting and research. But the Palestine I saw bore so little likeness to the stories I read, and so much resemblance to the systems I've known, that I am left believing that at least here, this objectivity is self-delusion. It's not that the facts of the stories are so wrong—though sometimes it is that—it is what is not said, the passive voice, the ceding of authority to military flacks, the elevation of factual complexity over self-evident morality.

This elevation of complexity over justice is part and parcel of the effort to forge a story of Palestine told solely by the colonizer, an effort that extends to the proscribing of boycotts by American states, the revocation of articles by journals, the expulsion of students from universities, the dismissal of news anchors by skittish networks, the shooting of journalists by army snipers, and the car-bombing of novelists by spy agencies. No other story, save one that enables theft, can be tolerated.

But there *are* other stories, and we who bankroll apartheid are more ignorant for not hearing them directly from storytellers like Deanna. I know that there are a lot of writers who believe they have access to a kind of artistic magic that allows them to inhabit any community in the world and write about it as if it is their own. I think those writers overestimate the power of their talent and intelligence, and underestimate how wisdom accrues over time, among nations and peoples, across ancestry. Even my words here, this bid for reparation, is a stranger's story—one told by a man still dazzled